This book was very loved
But we needed room for new.
We hope you will enj͟
Just as much as we ͟

NEW HAVEN FREE PUBLIC LIB

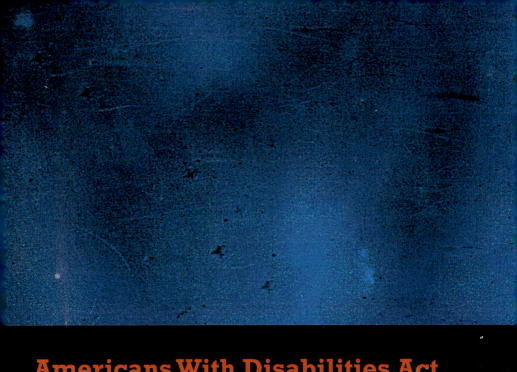

Americans With Disabilities Act

LANDMARK LEGISLATION

Americans With Disabilities Act

Susan Dudley Gold

Marshall Cavendish
Benchmark
New York

Dedicated to Steve LaRiviere, who rides a mean chair.

With special thanks to Kathryn McInnis–Misenor for her tremendous contributions to this book and to the campaign for the rights of people with disabilities nationwide. With thanks to Catherine McGlone, Esq., for her expert review of this manuscript.

Other Marshall Cavendish Offices:
Marshall Cavendish International (Asia) Private Limited, 1 New Industrial Road, Singapore 536196 • Marshall Cavendish International (Thailand) Co. Ltd. 253 Asoke, 12th Flr, Sukhumvit 21 Road, Klongtoey Nua, Wattana, Bangkok 10110, Thailand • Marshall Cavendish (Malaysia) Sdn Bhd, Times Subang, Lot 46, Subang Hi-Tech Industrial Park, Batu Tiga, 40000 Shah Alam, Selangor Darul Ehsan, Malaysia
Marshall Cavendish is a trademark of Times Publishing Limited

All websites were available and accurate when this book was sent to press.

Library of Congress Cataloging-in-Publication Data
Gold, Susan Dudley.
Americans with Disabilities Act / by Susan Dudley Gold.
p. cm.
ISBN 978-1-60870-039-4
1. People with disabilities—Legal status, laws, etc.—United States—Juvenile literature.
2. Discrimination against people with disabilities—Law and legislation—United States—Juvenile literature. 3. United States. Americans with Disabilities Act of 1990—Juvenile literature. I. Title.
KF480.G648 2001
342.7308'7—dc22
2009031195

Publisher: Michelle Bisson
Art Director: Anahid Hamparian
Series Designer: Sonia Chaghatzbanian
Photo research by Candlepants, Inc.

Cover photo: A group of disabled people walked or rode their wheelchairs in a march from the White House to the Capitol Building to draw support for the Americans with Disabilities Act.

The photographs in this book are used by permission and through the courtesy of: Jeff Markowitz/AP Images: cover; AP Images: 2, 33; Barry Thumma: 6; John Rous: 34; Amy Sancetta: 73; Jeff Markowitz: 95; JP: 106; Elaine Thompson: 108; Corbis, Bettmann: 3, 19, 28, 45, 60; Kathryn McInnis-Misenor: 14; Perkins School for the Blind, Watertown, MA: 24, 25; George H. W. Bush Presidential Library: 55; Disability Rights Education & Defense Fund: 63; Gallaudet University Library: 75; American Association of People with Disabilities, Yoshiko Dart: 80.

Printed in Malaysia(T)
1 3 5 6 4 2

Contents

President George H. W. Bush signs the Americans with Disabilities Act during a ceremony on the South Lawn of the White House on July 26, 1990. Joining the president were the Reverend Harold Wilke, rear left; chairman of the Equal Opportunity Employment Commission Evan Kemp Jr., left; Sandra Swift Parrino, chairwoman of the National Council on Disability, rear right; and Justin Dart Jr., chair of the President's Committee on the Employment of People with Disabilities, right.

Another Independence Day

When President George H. W. Bush signed the Americans with Disabilities Act (ADA) into law on July 26, 1990, some likened the legislation to the Emancipation Proclamation. The law established the rights of 43 million Americans with disabilities to hold jobs, enter buildings, seek education, ride buses and trains, participate in government, and be informed about matters relating to themselves. For many of the three thousand people sitting on the White House lawn that day to witness the signing, the law was the culmination of a years-long battle against discrimination. Some had been turned away from public schools as youngsters; others had been barred from public hearings and performances; still others had been warehoused in institutions isolated from the rest of society.

The passage of the ADA represented a dramatic shift in public policy toward those with disabilities. Until then, most government programs had treated Americans with disabilities as dependent and damaged human beings incapable of caring for themselves. This perspective reflected the view of many able-bodied Americans toward those with disabilities. Shortly after the passage of the ADA, Justin Dart Jr., a disabilities rights activist and a leader in the ADA campaign, described the attitude that encouraged discrimination against Americans with disabilities. "Our society," Dart noted, "is still infected by an insidious, now almost subconscious assumption that people with disabilities are less than fully human, and therefore are not fully eligible for the opportunities, services, and support systems which are available to other people as a matter of right."

For the first time, the law officially recognized that Americans with disabilities were citizens entitled to all the rights guaranteed in the Constitution. "As disabled," Dart observed, "we had to back up and get ourselves declared citizens first before we got our resources and our rights."

The ADA relied on the Civil Rights Act of 1964 and the Rehabilitation Act of 1973 in setting up procedures to enforce the law. The Equal Employment Opportunity Commission (EEOC) was given responsibility for issuing regulations and administering Title I. Title IV fell under the jurisdiction of the Federal Communications Commission. The U.S. attorney general and the Department of Transportation shared the duty of implementing Title II and Title III.

Thousands of people across the country with and without disabilities worked for years on the campaign for civil rights. They managed to hold off President Ronald Reagan's proposals to roll back government enforcement of previous laws that had furthered their cause. Realizing the need for a new law that would guarantee civil rights, they drafted the terms of the Americans with Disabilities Act, then wrote letters to newspapers, protested in the streets, lobbied Congress, knocked on doors, and talked with their fellow citizens to win support for the landmark legislation. The push for the ADA involved one of the largest coalitions of organizations and individuals in American history. At the signing of the ADA, President Bush described the alliance as "a strong and inspiring coalition of people who have shared both a dream and a passionate determination to make that dream come true."

By enacting the ADA, Congress put society on notice that discrimination against people because of their disabilities would no longer be tolerated. One of the act's main purposes, as detailed in the legislation, was "to provide a clear and comprehensive national mandate for the elimination of discrimination against individuals with disabilities." The ADA also included specific requirements to tear down the barriers that had blocked access to employment, education, public accommodations, and transportation.

President Bush praised the act as "the world's first comprehensive declaration of the equality for people with disabilities." He said the signing ceremony marked "another 'Independence Day,' one that is long overdue." As he put pen to paper, the president told the cheering spectators, "With today's signing of the landmark Americans [with] Disabilities Act, every man, woman, and child with a disability can now pass through once-closed doors into a bright new era of equality, independence and freedom." He concluded with the stirring words, "Let the shameful wall of exclusion finally come tumbling down."

During the first decade of the twenty-first century, Congress fought back efforts by business lobbyists and the administration of President George W. Bush—son of President George H. W. Bush—to ease some requirements in the ADA. Congress also passed new legislation to override Supreme

ADA of 1990

The Americans with Disabilities Act of 1990, passed by Congress on July 12 and 13, 1990, aimed to

(1) provide a national mandate to eliminate discrimination against people with disabilities;

(2) provide clear, strong, consistent, enforceable standards;

(3) ensure that the Federal Government played a central role in enforcing the standards; and

(4) invoke the sweep of congressional authority in order to address the major areas of discrimination faced daily by people with disabilities.

The law's five separate sections detailed the areas in which discrimination against people with disabilities would be prohibited:

Title I: Employment.

The law barred employers from discriminating against qualified people because of their disabilities. The section covered job applications, hiring and firing, promotions, wages, job training, and other terms of employment.

Title II: Public services.

Under this section, public transportation (other than some airplanes and some trains) had to be made accessible to people with disabilities. The law applied to public entities and private businesses operating such services for the public. It required that stations, bus stops, and other facilities also be made accessible.

Title III: Public accommodations and services operated by private entities.

This section required commercial buildings and facilities that served the public to be accessible to those in wheelchairs and others with disabilities. Included were hotels and motels, restaurants and bars, theaters and concert halls, auditoriums, retail stores, banks, gas stations, hospitals, professional offices, museums, libraries, parks and zoos, schools, gyms, golf courses, and many other places serving the public. The law required businesses to remove barriers that prevented people with disabilities from entering company buildings or participating in company services. If the removal of barriers was not "readily achievable," then businesses had to provide services to people with disabilities in other ways.

Title IV: Telecommunications.

The law required telephone companies to set up special communications services for people who were hearing-impaired, deaf, or speech-impaired. The cost of setting up the special service would be covered by a surcharge to all users of the telephone system. Title IV also obligated government-financed public service announcements on television to include written captions.

Title V: Miscellaneous provisions.

The last section covered a host of rules governing the administration of the law. It also protected from retaliation those who reported violations of the law.

Court decisions that weakened the ADA. These decisions had narrowed the definitions of disabilities under the ADA and decreased the measures required to accommodate workers with disabilities. Today, the law remains a strong deterrent to the rampant discrimination that once barred people with disabilities from jobs, housing, public facilities, public transportation, and communications systems. Although some discrimination and barriers still exist, the law changed the way society viewed people with disabilities. In doing so, it ensured that future generations will see people with disabilities as entitled to the same rights as other Americans. Children will grow up in a society that protects equal rights for people with and without disabilities.

A blind person vacationing in Hawaii, a deaf person calling to order pizza, a person in a wheelchair going to the movies or attending college—these have become commonplace, no longer eliciting comments or even surprise. Because of the ADA, doors have opened and those with disabilities have walked or rolled through. People with disabilities have become an integral part of American life.

The ADA "is not a law about disabilities," Mark Obatake, executive director of Hawaii Centers for Independent Living, told a reporter ten years after Congress enacted the legislation. "This is a law—like every other piece of civil rights legislation—about how, as a nation, a state, a community, we can embrace our differences."

One ADA Warrior's Story

Sitting in her wheelchair on the White House lawn among others who helped win passage of the Americans with Disabilities Act, Kathryn McInnis could not keep from smiling. She and her mother, Jean McInnis, had taken the train from Maine to attend the ceremony marking the signing of the ADA. Jean told her daughter to relish the moment. Kathryn celebrated the historic event with delight, accompanied by her mother and a friend, disability rights activist Tom Andrews, who later became a member of Congress. "For all [the bill's] flaws, the ADA was amazing," Kathryn McInnis said later. "It was all about being a citizen and taking responsibility for our civil rights."

Kathryn McInnis did not start out as a political activist for people with disabilities. Her story contains many of the same challenges faced by others involved in the ADA campaign: disability, discrimination, frustration, and at times a sense of futility. And like the others, she used her own resources—

Jean McInnis gives her daughter, Kathryn McInnis, in wheelchair, a congratulatory hug on the White House lawn after the signing of the Americans With Disabilities Act, which Kathryn helped write.

courage, determination, and hard work—to overcome the barriers.

The sixth of twelve children, McInnis began her long journey as a person with a disability at age six, when she was diagnosed with juvenile rheumatoid arthritis. By age eleven she required a wheelchair to get around. Officials at her elementary school decided it was unsafe for her to continue attending school there. Instead, Jean McInnis began tutoring her young daughter at home. Later, tutors paid by the city school system took over teaching duties for the bright youngster.

By the time Kathryn reached high school age, her mother worried about her becoming isolated from other teens. She began lobbying for Kathryn to attend the local high school. School officials were skeptical. Steep stone steps led up to the entrance of the nineteenth-century brick school building. Undaunted, Jean McInnis—a sports enthusiast who cheered her other children at various games—persuaded the football team to carry the slim girl and her wheelchair into and out of the school each day. Kathryn graduated with high honors and later earned the school's distinguished alumni award for her work to advance equality for oppressed people.

A RIGHT, NOT A PRIVILEGE

Descended from a family of activists who had joined the suffragettes and stood up to the Ku Klux Klan, McInnis learned early about politics and taking stands on issues that counted. Her "fearless" mother—who had no problem pushing her daughter's wheelchair into restaurants even after being told not to enter—provided firsthand lessons in taking action to overcome problems. "History," Kathryn observed later, "is about the actions of regular people standing up and saying, 'I have a right to this.'"

In her teens, McInnis worked on several political campaigns in her hometown of Saco, Maine, including her sister's successful run for school board. Soon Kathryn was running her own campaign. At twenty-one she became the youngest woman, and one of a handful of politicians with disabilities in the nation, to win election to city council. Her election, in 1980, ignited an ugly dispute over access to public meetings. The Saco council held its meetings in the second-floor auditorium in City Hall, and the 1856 brick building had no elevator.

McInnis asked that council meetings be held in a nearby school to allow her and others with disabilities to attend. A majority of the council voted against McInnis's request. Several councilors argued that the city's meetings should be conducted in their traditional place in City Hall, the seat of municipal government. One councilor contended that McInnis had created the problem for herself by winning the election. "We didn't ask her to run," he told a reporter for the local newspaper, the *Journal Tribune*. "She knew that she'd have trouble getting into City Hall if she won ... it's her problem." He insisted that the city had no obligation to make the meeting place accessible to McInnis and that she should have "realized her position" in society as a person with a disability. When asked if his comments applied to all people with disabilities, he replied, "If I were handicapped, I wouldn't serve in government. . . . You can't get into the buildings."

McInnis had to rely on a relative to carry her up two flights of stairs (at least twenty steps) to be sworn into office. After the council's vote against her request, she made it clear, in a letter to the local newspaper, that she intended to continue her campaign for access. "I am aware every day of physical barriers that limit my freedom of movement," she wrote. "My

Rehabilitation Act of 1973

Public Law 93-112, 93rd Congress, H. R. 8070
September 26, 1973

Employment Under Federal Contracts

SEC. 503 (excerpt). (a) Any contract in excess of $2,500 entered into by any Federal department or agency for the procurement of personal property and nonpersonal services (including construction) for the United States shall contain a provision requiring that, in employing persons to carry out such contract the party contracting with the United States shall take affirmative action to employ and advance in employment qualified handicapped individuals. . . .

Nondiscrimination Under Federal Grants

SEC. 504. No otherwise qualified handicapped individual in the United States, as defined in section 7(6), shall, solely by reason of his handicap, be excluded from the participation in, be denied the benefits of, or be subjected to discrimination under any program or activity receiving Federal financial assistance.

freedom is dependent on others' compassion. And freedom that is dependent on anything is not true freedom. I am only asking what is my right, not my privilege."

The council's actions and comments drew a barrage of criticism from enraged citizens. Letter writers assailed the council's position. One suggested a ban on the entire city until officials opened the council meetings to everyone. Another noted that President Franklin D. Roosevelt had not let his "position" as a person with a disability deter him from running for office. The *Journal Tribune* chastised councilors for their "deplorable lack of compassion and understanding" and their "less than enlightened reaction" to the lack of access. Not only was the council guilty of insensitivity, the paper said, it was also violating state and federal laws. The Federal Rehabilitation Act of 1973 required that citizens have access to the deliberations of boards that decided how public funds would be spent. In addition, the Maine Human Rights Act required employers to provide equal access to jobs. McInnis, the paper noted, was an employee of the city of Saco, receiving $300 a year for her service as city councilor.

Even with such laws in place, however, the problem of access persisted, according to the paper, because society still harbored biased views about people with disabilities. The uproar in Saco, the editorial writer contended, reflected society's attitude "that until very recently called for keeping all handicapped people as far out of sight as possible. Handicapped people were and still too often are treated as though they were lepers."

At the council's next meeting, a one-vote majority approved McInnis's motion to meet at a local school until the city could renovate a downstairs room as council chambers. Three of the city's seven councilors voted against the measure. In making the proposal, McInnis gave an impassioned speech about the rights of people with disabilities. "The opportunity to contribute to our culture, our nation, should not be limited to the young and/or able-bodied," she told her fellow councilors. "The integration of handicapped and elderly people into the life of the community could only serve to benefit our

Franklin D. Roosevelt was almost never photographed in a way that showed him using crutches or a wheelchair. This photo of FDR at the New York State Democratic Convention in 1926 is a rare exception.

society—a society that for too long has either isolated handicapped and elderly people or restricted them from contributing to their communities."

CREATING HISTORY

The controversy won McInnis national attention. She was interviewed by the *Boston Globe* and by Larry King, then a popular radio show host, and received a call of support from Andrew Young, a prominent civil rights activist and leader of the Democratic Party. The incident also brought her to the attention of the Maine Association of Handicapped Persons (MAHP), a nonprofit organization that had recently switched its focus from obtaining social services for people with disabilities to campaigning for their civil rights. Officials of the group invited McInnis to attend a meeting. Her battle, they told her, was their battle.

For McInnis and the MAHP, the fight had just begun. As a board member and later as president and political organizer for the group, McInnis played a key role in the campaign to make Maine's city buses accessible to people with disabilities. She and others worked to open public buildings to patrons with disabilities, pushed for increased educational opportunities for children with disabilities, helped write portions of the Americans with Disabilities Act, and lobbied for its passage. When Congress finally enacted the ADA, McInnis and the other warriors who had worked so long and hard to win civil rights for people with disabilities became a part of the American story. Recalled McInnis, "All of us who were there the day it passed felt that we had created history."

CHAPTER TWO

A History of Abuse

For centuries, people with disabilities were treated differently, and often far less charitably, than those without disabilities. A person's disability—whether it was blindness, deafness, dwarfism, inability to walk, or some other condition—set him or her apart from society's view of what was "normal." In earlier times, superstition or religion led people to believe that disabilities were the devil's work. Those who had disabilities, they believed, were either dangerous or being punished for evil acts.

As a result of those beliefs, some cultures banished, ridiculed, persecuted, or killed people with disabilities. When Europeans settled colonies in North America, several of their charters specifically excluded people with disabilities. They assumed such people would be a drain on the community.

Beginning in the mid–1600s American colonists established almshouses, or poorhouses, to provide food and shelter for those unable to care for themselves. People with physical or mental disabilities were among those served by the institutions. Conditions in the houses varied, but most were unpleasant and unsanitary. A report prepared by the New York Senate in 1856 described that state's almshouses as "the most disgraceful memorials of public charity." According to the report, the institutions were plagued by "filth, nakedness, licentiousness, general bad morals ... [and] gross neglect of the most ordinary comforts and decencies of life."

Society viewed people disabled by war wounds more charitably. Early American colonies provided for soldiers and sailors injured during battle. By 1865, following the Civil War, Congress was providing pensions for almost 2 million poor people and veterans with disabilities. After the Civil War, Congress also established institutional homes providing room and board and some medical care for destitute veterans throughout the nation.

INSTITUTIONS FOR PEOPLE WITH DISABILITIES

By the 1820s reformers had begun setting up institutions to meet the special needs of people with mental and physical disabilities. At first these institutions taught people trades that allowed many to return to their communities, where they supported themselves with help from their families. During the tough economic times that followed the Civil War, however, jobs dried up and families were unable to provide assistance. As a result, many people with disabilities remained in institutions, sometimes for life. Samuel Gridley Howe, a doctor and director of the nation's first school for blind children, decried the trend toward permanent residence. In 1866 he urged that those with disabilities "should be kept diffused among sound and normal persons." He believed people with disabilities should take their place

Laura Bridgman's Education

Laura Bridgman, born in Hanover, New Hampshire, in 1829, was two when scarlet fever left her blind and deaf, with no speech and little sense of smell. Her mother taught her to knit and to do various chores around the farmhouse where she lived, but she received no schooling. Dr. Samuel Howe, director of the New England Asylum for the Blind in Massachusetts, learned of her in 1837.

That October Laura's parents enrolled her in Howe's institute. There she lived with Howe and his sister, returning home to New Hampshire for visits from time to time. Dr. Howe came to describe her as "cheerful and even gay and frolicsome. . . . There are few persons so lighthearted, so cheery, so full of mirth, so ready at any moment to laugh at a joke or join in a game at romps."

One of Laura's first accomplishments was to recognize Howe's sign for figs, a fruit she particularly liked. To teach her signs for the letters of the alphabet required a much more detailed plan. Howe began by attaching paper labels with raised lettering to several common items. By using her sense of touch, Laura learned to "read" each label and soon could correctly match a word in raised letters to the item it identified. Then Howe separated the letters of a word and showed Laura how to piece them together. After weeks of effort, the young girl perceived that she could use the letters to spell out her own words. In much the same way, Laura mastered numbers and punctuation. In later sessions she learned how to sign letters and words with her fingers and to interpret them when someone else traced them out on her hand.

Teachers at the school also taught Laura how to write by guiding her hand to form each letter with a pencil. She

The New England Asylum for the Blind, where Laura Bridgman received her education, was among the first that prepared blind people to become productive members of society.

later kept a journal and wrote many letters to friends and family. Laura's accomplishments amazed the public, who came to view the children and the school at weekly exhibitions. Howe's extensive reports on Laura's education and progress—published in several languages—gained worldwide attention and helped change the way educators taught students with disabilities. Laura became even more of a celebrity when British author Charles Dickens wrote about her in his book *American Notes,* an account of his travels in the United States in 1842. Laura's accomplishments helped alter people's perceptions of those with disabilities

Laura Bridgman lost her sight, hearing, and ability to speak when she came down with scarlet fever at age two. By teaching Laura to write and communicate using signs and raised letters (the precursor of braille), Samuel G. Howe of the New England Asylum for the Blind opened up the world to people with hearing and sight disabilities forever.

and showed that students with disabilities could learn and benefit from education.

Anne Sullivan, a graduate of the institute who was herself visually impaired, studied Howe's work with Laura Bridgman before taking on the responsibility of teaching the young Helen Keller, also blind and deaf. Sullivan's success in teaching Helen how to communicate won worldwide recognition and was later detailed in the play and movie *The Miracle Worker*. Like Laura Bridgman, Helen Keller served as a strong role model for people with disabilities everywhere.

in society, not be forced to live apart from those without disabilities. Whenever possible, he argued, children with disabilities should be educated alongside other students. Only when they needed special attention not available in public schools should students with disabilities be taught in institutions. Howe believed that once these students acquired skills, they should be encouraged to live and work outside such institutions.

Howe spent most of his professional career as a doctor helping people with disabilities overcome obstacles. Born in Boston in 1801, he became the era's leading spokesman for the rights of those with physical or mental disabilities. Unlike others of his generation who believed that people with disabilities could be given only charity and pity, Howe pushed for education and training for those with disabilities. "Much can be done for them," he said of the blind students educated at the New England Asylum for the Blind (later Perkins School for the Blind). "You may give [the blind man] the means of becoming an enlightened, happy, and useful member of society; you may give him and his fellow-blind the means of earning their own livelihood, or at least of doing much towards it; you may light the lamp of knowledge within them."

He was among the first to suggest full-time, professional jobs for blind workers, as teachers of languages and other courses, as ministers, as counselors, and as employees in a number of other fields. He also recognized that the greatest obstacle to educating blind children was not their disability but the coddling of well-meaning relatives. Such treatment, he said, interfered with the development of the children's other senses.

A PEOPLE APART

Many people, including a number of leading health professionals, did not share Howe's vision of independence for people with disabilities. Charitable organizations that formed in America in the late 1800s promoted "taking care of" people with disabilities. Although these organizations advanced humane treatment of people with disabilities, their paternalistic outlook often led to the segregation of those with disabilities from the rest of society. Under the care of these organizations, people with disabilities attended special programs instead of public schools, and many lived in institutions apart from their families.

A famous showman furthered the view that those with disabilities were different from other people. Beginning in the 1830s P. T. Barnum astounded audiences with his exhibits of unusual characters, including dwarfs (which he billed as midgets), conjoined twins, bearded ladies, and others disfigured or marked by physical disabilities. Tom Thumb, among the most famous of Barnum's dwarf performers, and others in the freak shows earned considerable income from the exhibits. But the shows set these people apart from society and made them the objects of curiosity. Today most dwarfs —or Little People as some prefer to be known—strongly object to being called midgets. Even though Barnum operated his circus in the 1800s, Little People today still associate the word *midget* with freak shows and the demeaning effects of being put on display.

Those with disabilities continued to be set apart well into the twentieth century. Their physical problems became barriers that separated them from the rest of society. During the 1930s and 1940s the Nazis under Adolf Hitler persecuted deaf people and those with disabilities, sterilized and

Circus showman P. T. Barnum poses with Charles Sherwood Stratton, the dwarf he renamed General Tom Thumb. Even though Barnum's show made Stratton a wealthy man, many people believed putting him on public display was demeaning and resent the term *midget*, used at the time to describe people of unusually short stature. Some prefer the term *dwarf*, while others use *Little People*.

killed people with disabilities, and barred marriage or sexual contact with people who had either a mental or physical disability.

In the 1960s sociologist Erving Goffman wrote about the stigma of disabilities in a groundbreaking book that explored prejudice and discrimination against people who had disabilities. The book, *Stigma: Notes on the Management of Spoiled Identity*, revealed that people with disabilities were targets of discrimination just as women, black Americans, and other minorities were. This presented a new way of viewing people with disabilities—as a distinct group whose civil rights were being trampled—and ultimately helped lay the groundwork for the passage of the Americans with Disabilities Act.

Nondisabled people often treated those with disabilities with disrespect and disapproval or simply ignored them, Goffman reported. People shouted at those who were blind, as if losing their sight had somehow also impaired their hearing; they treated those in wheelchairs as if they had lost the capacity to think along with the ability to walk. Kathryn McInnis recalled being ignored by servers in restaurants. "They would never look me in the face," McInnis related. They spoke only to her mother, who accompanied her. After McInnis ordered for herself, servers often asked her mother if Kathryn could eat the food or drink she had requested.

Others viewed those with disabilities as curiosities, rather than as people with feelings. They stared at people with disabilities or asked them inappropriately personal questions. When McInnis was pregnant with her daughter, strangers asked her how she had conceived and how she planned to give birth.

As members of society, many people with disabilities shared the public's views of what was normal and what was not. They, too, tended to see themselves as damaged, weak beings who were not normal and, therefore, not worthy of fair treatment. The resulting self-hate and shame at being less than normal, in their own eyes as well as in the eyes of others, further sidelined people with disabilities. Even McInnis, a fierce fighter for rights since her teens, fell victim to self-doubts. "I always knew about rights," but at times, she acknowledged, "I thought I was not good enough."

Franklin D. Roosevelt:

A memorial erected in the nation's capital in 1997 to commemorate President Franklin D. Roosevelt sparked a heated debate over whether he should be depicted truthfully, in a wheelchair, or whether he should be immortalized as the "cured cripple" that he pretended to be in public. In 1921 Roosevelt was stricken with polio. The disease left him paralyzed from the waist down. At the time, many Americans believed that people in wheelchairs and those with other disabilities were not fit to carry on normal lives, work, or contribute to society—and certainly not vigorous enough to lead a nation on its knees in the wake of the Great Depression. For that reason, Roosevelt concealed his paralysis from the American public when he ran for office and served as the nation's thirty-second president. He taught himself to walk short distances using a cane or crutches and tight-fitting iron leg braces concealed under his pants, gripped a lectern to hold himself upright when he made speeches, and supported himself on an aide's arm when standing in public. He almost never appeared publicly in a wheelchair, and most people had the impression that the president had recovered.

Despite protests from Americans with disabilities and others, the original memorial did not portray Roosevelt in a wheelchair. Instead, it included a bas relief of Roosevelt riding in a car and a sculpture of him seated in a chair and wearing a cape. Only by looking at the back of the statue would a viewer discover that the chair had wheels. Members of the memorial commission asserted that because Roosevelt sought to keep the extent of his disability a secret during his lifetime, portraying him in a wheelchair would be historically inaccurate.

President in a Wheelchair

But disability rights activists argued that Roosevelt had served as a powerful role model to people with disabilities during his lifetime and afterward. By not showing him as he was, they contended, the memorial ignored an important part of his life and deprived those with disabilities of a powerful symbol of "strength and inspiration."

In 1998 the National Park Service agreed to add a sculpture of Roosevelt that clearly showed his inability to walk. The National Organization on Disability raised the $1.65 million needed to erect the statue of the president in a wheelchair resembling the one he used as president. President Bill Clinton presided at the dedication of the new artwork in January 2001. "This is a monument to freedom," he told the celebrants gathered at the memorial; "the power of every man and woman to transcend circumstance, to laugh in the face of fate, to make the most of what God has given."

SOLDIERS WITH DISABILITIES DEMAND MORE

The United States' involvement in two world wars—from 1917 to 1918 and 1941 to 1945—added almost 900,000 wounded soldiers to the rolls of Americans with disabilities. These soldiers expected more than disability payments. They insisted that they had a right to jobs and a chance to participate in the American dream. They encountered the same dilemma confronting black soldiers after World War II. They had fought for America's freedom, yet these men came home to find their own freedoms blocked by discrimination.

Determined veterans with disabilities began lobbying for their share of the pie. During World War II, Congress passed a law, the Disabled Veterans' Rehabilitation Act of 1943, which provided job training for 621,000 veterans with disabilities. The act applied to all veterans with disabilities whose service began on or after December 7, 1941, the date Japan attacked Pearl Harbor and drew the United States into the war. In 1944 Congress authorized a GI Bill of Rights that offered, among other benefits, free college tuition and a monthly living allowance for all veterans. Many soldiers, including those with disabilities, took advantage of the programs. However, in too many cases, soldiers with disabilities met other barriers that prevented them from participating. Kenneth Sawtelle, who lost both legs after stepping on a mine during World War II, signed up for classes at a local college. When he arrived on the first day, he discovered he would have to climb a long staircase to enter the building. With prosthetic legs, braces, and canes, he saw no way of overcoming the barrier. "I had to give up that dream," he said later.

Years later, a soldier wounded in the Vietnam War described the situation facing him when he returned from overseas: Paralyzed and in a wheelchair, Charles Sabatier Jr. could not

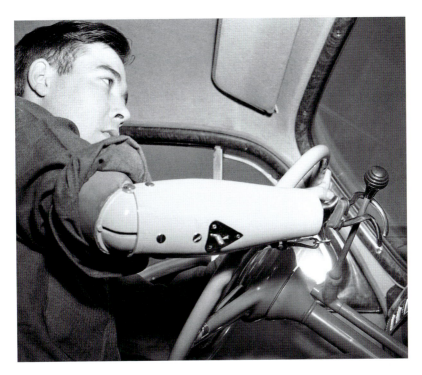

Private Aziza Remington, who lost his right arm in World War II, demonstrates how he learned to shift gears using his prosthetic right arm.

get out of his house, had no way of boarding the city bus, could not ride along the sidewalks of his town because of the curbs, and faced discrimination when trying to find a job. The experience made him realize that he had fought for others' freedom but not his own. He later led the fight to win equality for people with disabilities as director of the Paralyzed Veterans of America and of the Boston Commission for Persons with Disabilities.

Veterans with disabilities were among the first to assert that discrimination and other barriers blocking their access to programs violated their civil rights. These returning soldiers led the chorus of voices demanding fair treatment for people with disabilities.

President Lyndon B. Johnson signs a bill to provide preschool educational programs for children with disabilities on September 30, 1968. Johnson was an early advocate for rights for people with disabilities.

CHAPTER THREE

First Steps Toward Civil Rights

The campaign for civil rights waged by black Americans in the 1950s and 1960s inspired many people with disabilities to fight their own battle against discrimination. The Civil Rights Act of 1964 was the first major piece of legislation in a century to tackle discrimination against black Americans. Although the act did not address the rights of people with disabilities, it did establish the framework for dealing with discrimination cases. The rules and structure set up by the 1964 law became the framework for subsequent laws—including the Americans with Disabilities Act— that advanced the rights of people with disabilities. In many ways the fight for disability rights would mirror the earlier struggle of black Americans. People with disabilities would seek to integrate schools, push to desegregate public buildings, and lobby to ban discrimination at the workplace.

President Lyndon Johnson helped launch the campaign for disability rights in 1968 when he signed the Architectural

Barriers Act. The legislation required new or renovated buildings used or financed by the federal government to be accessible to those with disabilities. The act was the first official recognition by Congress of the physical barriers faced by people with disabilities. The new law served more as a suggestion than a requirement, however. With little enforcement power, it did not have the clout needed to open public buildings to people who could not walk up stairs or negotiate narrow passageways.

THE CIVIL RIGHTS ACT FOR DISABLED PEOPLE

A big breakthrough came in 1973 with the passage of what became known as the Civil Rights Act for Disabled People. Based on a similar provision in the Civil Rights Act of 1964, Section 504 of the Rehabilitation Act of 1973 barred discrimination based on a person's disabilities. For the first time federal legislation linked the discrimination and barriers faced by Americans with disabilities to a loss of their civil rights. In passing the bill, Congress recognized that inaccessible buildings and buses, separate classrooms, unemployment, and lack of communications systems for deaf people were not unavoidable results of being disabled. Instead the law identified such situations as a civil rights issue. People with disabilities were being discriminated against and deprived of their civil rights.

Advocates of the historic bill faced an uphill battle in winning its passage. A Democratic Congress first passed a rehabilitation bill in October 1972 that would have shifted the focus of vocational training programs to help more people with severe disabilities. It also would have set up independent-living centers to enable people with disabilities to move out of institutions and participate more fully in the community.

Republican president Richard Nixon vetoed the bill, saying it would cost too much money and that its requirements would interfere with the right of states to manage their own social programs. When the president announced his decision, Congress had already adjourned and therefore could not override the veto.

Activists with disabilities wasted no time in expressing their outrage over the president's veto. In New York City protesters in wheelchairs and on crutches blocked traffic and closed off Madison Avenue for nearly an hour during the evening rush hour to express their support of the bill. A spokesperson for the activists said the group had organized the protest to make the public "aware of the plight of the handicapped."

The following March Congress passed a similar bill that would have set aside $2.6 billion for programs to aid people with physical and mental disabilities. One of the bill's supporters speculated that the popularity of the cause would persuade the Republican president to sign the legislation this time. "After all," he told the *New York Times*, "there can't be too many folks who want to go on record as opposing aid to the crippled." Again Nixon vetoed the bill, and Congress upheld the veto. The *Times* called the president's act "a hollow victory," won "at the expense of the weakest and most impoverished elements of society."

Finally Congress submitted a scaled-down version of the bill that called for $1.54 billion over two years for programs for people with disabilities. Nixon signed the bill on September 26, 1973. Although the bill allocated much less money than the previous two had, it contained a provision that would shake up the disability rights movement as none before. Hailed as the civil rights act of people with disabilities, the revised Rehabilitation Act of 1973—in Section 504—barred discrimination based on physical and mental disabilities. The amendment, introduced by Democratic senator Hubert Humphrey of Minnesota and Republican senator Charles Percy of Illinois, put Congress on record that discrimination against Americans with disabilities would no longer be tolerated, at least not when federal dollars were involved.

In addition the act—in Section 501—required federal agencies to set up programs to hire and promote workers with disabilities, including ways of adapting work sites to allow people with disabilities to hold jobs. The act also required—in Section 503—that employers take "affirmative action" to hire and promote qualified workers with disabilities for jobs on federally funded projects of more than $2,500. The bill allocated funding for rehabilitation and job training programs for people with disabilities. In addition it set aside money to build new rehabilitation centers and help fund renovations to public buildings to make them accessible to those who had difficulty walking.

A person with a disability, as defined by the law, was one who had "a physical or mental disability which . . . constitutes or results in a substantial handicap to employment and [who] can reasonably be expected to benefit in terms of employability from vocational rehabilitation services provided [by] this act." In 1974 Congress expanded the definition to: "[A]ny person who (i) has a physical or mental impairment which substantially limits one or more major life activities, (ii) has a record of such an impairment, or (iii) is regarded as having such an impairment." The last section, in particular, was an important addition to the law because it protected people who were not disabled by their condition but who were discriminated against by employers and others because of it. In some cases, companies had fired or refused to hire people who had recovered from cancer or other diseases.

UNITED, WE PROTEST

The battle to win passage of the rehabilitation act united the various segments of the disabilities rights movement. Until then, people had tended to divide into organizations serving their particular disability; blind people united under one umbrella; those with impaired hearing formed groups focused on deafness; and people with other disabilities set up their own associations. With the passage of the Rehabilitation Act of 1973, all people with disabilities had a common goal: to ensure that their civil rights were protected. The various organizations began reaching out to every segment of the community of people with disabilities. For the first time, people with all types of disabilities were seen as a minority group, by themselves as well as by others.

The celebration over the passage of the act was short-lived. While Americans with disabilities rejoiced in the bill's promise to end discrimination, they soon realized that little had changed. From 1975 to 1977 workers with disabilities filed 3,500 complaints with the Department of Labor relating to job discrimination. As a result, workers with disabilities collected $300,000 in back pay. Only 20 percent of the complaints, however, were considered. The commission hearing the disputes threw out the rest. Without meaningful regulations to enforce the law's provisions, its goal of defeating discrimination could not begin to be accomplished. Congress assigned the task of setting up the new regulations to the U.S. Department of Health, Education, and Welfare (HEW). It took the department four years to issue the rules.

During the long campaign to implement the law, people in

the disability rights movement united to take on the establishment. Together, Americans with disabilities, parents of children with disabilities, and their supporters lobbied Congress, filed lawsuits, led protests, and wrote letters to win enactment of tough antidiscrimination regulations. In July 1976 the federal district court of the District of Columbia ruled in the case of *Cherry* v. *Mathews* that the government had delayed too long. Judge John L. Smith ordered HEW to develop and release the regulations immediately.

Working with HEW officials, a wide-ranging coalition of people with disabilities worked on regulations for the law. These were submitted to F. David Mathews, secretary of Health, Education and Welfare, on January 12, 1977, just days before the administration of President-elect Jimmy Carter took office. Mathews asked Congress to review the new regulations, which led to another court case to speed up the release of the rules. When incoming HEW secretary Joseph A. Califano Jr. assumed office, the appeals court was reviewing the case. Califano asked for time to review the proposed regulations before releasing them.

Activists for disability rights feared that Califano might make major revisions to the regulations they had carefully negotiated with HEW. They urged him to sign the rules as proposed. "The Department's failure to issue regulations has meant that hundreds of thousands of intended beneficiaries of H.E.W.–funded programs throughout the country who are handicapped continue to be subjected to discrimination in employment, health and social services, education and access to programs," Daniel Yohalem, a member of the disability coalition, wrote to Califano.

In the spring of 1977 activists conducted sit-ins in HEW offices around the nation. The longest, a sit-in at the regional offices of HEW in San Francisco lasting nearly four weeks, gained wide publicity and put pressure on the Carter administration to act on the matter. Finally, on April 28, 1977, Secretary Califano signed the regulations to enforce Section 504's ban on discrimination against Americans with disabilities. Judith Heumann, who had organized the San Francisco sit-in, applauded the new rules. "We believe we have won the major issues," Heumann told a *New York Times* reporter.

The regulations barred employers receiving federal funds from discriminating against people with disabilities. Bosses also had to make "reasonable accommodations" to the workplace to enable employees with disabilities to do their jobs. The rules required public schools to open their doors and programs to students with disabilities. Schools and other public buildings had up to three years to make their facilities accessible to people with disabilities. Schools, colleges, hospitals, doctors' offices, and other institutions receiving public funds and built after June 1, 1977, also had to be accessible to those in wheelchairs. HEW officials estimated that it would cost companies a combined total of $2.4 billion a year to meet the law's requirements.

In signing the new regulations, Califano noted that the 1973 law reflected "the recognition of the Congress that most handicapped persons can lead proud and productive lives, despite their disabilities." He predicted that the action would "usher in a new era of equality for handicapped individuals in which unfair barriers to self-sufficiency and decent treatment will begin to fall before the force of law."

EDUCATION AND INSTITUTIONALIZATION

People with developmental disabilities and their advocates began their own campaign for human rights. They formed a coalition, the Consortium for Citizens with Developmental Disabilities (CCDD) and lobbied for laws that would protect the rights of those living in institutions. In 1975 Congress reauthorized the Developmental Disabilities Assistance and Bill of Rights Act, which required that those living in institutions be provided with the services they needed. The act also gave people with disabilities and their families the right to participate in planning treatment programs. A follow-up law, enacted in 1980, strengthened enforcement by giving the federal government the power to sue the operators of institutions that disregarded the rights of the people living there.

Also in 1975 Congress passed another civil rights law, the Education for All Handicapped Children Act, for children with disabilities. Since then, Congress has amended the law, now known as the Individuals with Disabilities Education Act (IDEA), many times. The law guaranteed the right of all American children to a "free appropriate public education," regardless of disability. According to U.S. government figures, in 1970 only 20 percent of America's children with disabilities received public school education. In many states, students who were deaf, blind, mentally retarded, or emotionally disturbed were barred by law from attending public schools.

Under the act, public schools had to provide free special education programs and other services to students with disabilities who needed them. In addition, school systems had to develop educational plans for every student in their district who had a disability. Parents had the right to participate in the planning and implementation of their children's educational programs. The law also stipulated that children with disabilities should be taught in the "least restrictive" classroom setting appropriate. The last requirement was included to discourage segregating pupils with disabilities from the general student population. According to the act, children with disabilities should be taught in regular class-rooms with nondisabled students whenever possible.

PROBLEMS PERSIST

With the adoption of regulations governing the Rehabilita-tion Act of 1973, the Department of Health, Education, and Welfare received more complaints about discrimination based on disability than about discrimination based on race and sex combined. During the first four months of 1978, the department processed 377 complaints from people with dis-abilities, about half relating to job discrimination.

Amendments to the Rehabilitation Act enacted in 1978 expanded its regulations against discrimination to cover fed-eral agencies, not just firms receiving federal funds. The new provisions also extended programs set up under the original law and added a community service employment program for people with disabilities.

Ten years after the Rehabilitation Act of 1973 became law, Americans with disabilities told pollster Louis Harris that their lives had improved as a result of the 1973 act. The nationwide poll, conducted in 1983 for the International Cen-ter for the Disabled in New York, reported that two-thirds of those polled said the law had provided more opportunities for them during the last decade. But it also revealed that pov-erty, discrimination, few jobs, little education, and fear con-tinued to plague people with disabilities. According to the results of the study, only 25 percent of Americans with dis-abilities had jobs even though two-thirds of those polled said they wanted to work. Half had an annual household income of less than $15,000. Forty percent did not have a high school diploma. Almost 60 percent told the pollsters that they did not go to movies, plays, or sports events "because their disability might cause them to get hurt or sick or be victimized by crime."

The one thousand people participating in the poll made it clear they wanted more. Three-quarters of them said that people with disabilities should have the same protections that other minorities possessed under civil rights laws. Rather than government programs, they wanted access to jobs to support themselves. Dr. Nina Hill, a director at the International Center for the Disabled, said many people believed that those with disabilities were "content to be supported by the government." The poll results, she said, showed "how untrue" such an assumption was.

NEW FEDERALISM, OLD BARRIERS

The election of Ronald Reagan as president in 1980 threatened to dismantle the hard-won gains that people with disabilities had made under the 1973 law. A conservative Republican, Reagan espoused a philosophy that he termed the "new federalism." He believed there should be fewer government controls on private business. Left alone, he surmised, businesses would flourish, which would benefit the economy and the nation as a whole. The poor and the disadvantaged would benefit from this prosperity far more than from government programs, Reagan contended. According to his theory, deregulation would wean people from their dependence on government programs and make them self-reliant.

In reality, however, the new system of deregulation endangered the efforts of people with disabilities to attain independence. Instead of removing barriers, new regulations

Picketers wear Ronald Reagan masks as they protest at a federal hearing held by the U.S. Department of Education on the president's plans to weaken regulations in the Handicapped Child Education Act of 1982.

proposed by federal regulators aimed to weaken the 1973 law and allow buses, buildings, jobs, and other arenas to remain inaccessible. Without federal prodding and incentives, private businesses had little inclination to pay to install systems that would accommodate people with disabilities.

With the Reagan administration's opposition to federal civil rights legislation and weak enforcement of existing federal regulations, many advocates for disability rights focused their efforts on the states. In Massachusetts disability rights groups helped win passage of an amendment to the state constitution that banned state programs from discriminating against people with disabilities. Activists seeking access to public buses in Michigan relied on that state's 1976 Handicappers' (later changed to Persons with Disabilities) Civil Rights Act, which mandated that public services be accessible to people with disabilities. In New York City, groups representing people with disabilities put together a plan in 1984 that would have provided elevators at some subway stations and wheelchair lifts in all new city buses. Mayor Edward Koch blocked the agreement, which would have cost $50 million over eight years. The mayor objected to the expense and proposed an alternative system that would provide specially equipped vans for use by people with disabilities. "To spend millions for elevators to satisfy a principle of station accessibility for the handicapped and yet not provide any real help for the handicapped, is very poor public policy," Koch told reporters. "I cannot accept it." Disappointed proponents of the plan charged that the mayor had "double-crossed the disabled community."

CHAPTER FOUR

The Campaign for Access

In the years leading up to the passage of the ADA, the campaign for disability rights had mixed results in court. Some decisions strengthened disability rights, while other rulings weakened them. The first major case to seek relief under Section 504 involved a student with a hearing impairment, Frances B. Davis, who wanted to attend nursing classes at Southeastern Community College in North Carolina. When the college rejected her application, she sued in U.S. District Court for eastern North Carolina, claiming the school had discriminated against her because of her disability.

Davis's lawyers maintained that she was "otherwise qualified" for the course and that Section 504 required the college to disregard her disability when determining whether to enroll her. The college argued that Davis's disability made it impossible for her to participate in the class or to provide safe care for patients. The case, *Southeastern Community College* v. *Davis*, made its way to the Supreme Court, and in 1979 the justices ruled unanimously against Davis. In making the decision, the Court concluded that Section 504 did not prevent schools from setting "legitimate physical requirements" necessary to perform a job or participate in a school program. The decision declared that an "otherwise qualified" student was one who could "meet all of a program's requirements in spite of his handicap." Furthermore, the Court ruled, Congress never meant to require institutions to make "extensive modifications" to ensure that people with disabilities could participate.

Disability rights activists and their supporters in Congress viewed the decision as a major setback. "I am deeply afraid that many colleges and universities will begin to look at the *Davis* case as giving them carte blanche to routinely deny supportive services to deaf and blind students," Frank Bowe, director of the American Coalition of Citizens with Disabilities, said after the ruling. Justice Lewis F. Powell Jr., author of the Supreme Court opinion, left some hope for future petitioners with disabilities, however. Noting that "the line between a lawful refusal to extend affirmative action and illegal discrimination" might be unclear, he speculated that some accommodations to assist people with disabilities could be made "without imposing undue financial and administrative burdens." In these cases, he suggested, a refusal to make such reasonable changes might be considered "unreasonable and discriminatory."

Meanwhile, colleges raised concerns that modifications for students with disabilities would lower standards. Disability rights proponents disagreed with that assessment. "We have found that most handicapped people need very little done in order for them to participate," said Martha Ross Redden, a director of projects for people with disabilities sponsored by several national organizations. "[W]e want institutions to hold to the very highest standards." The biggest problem, both sides agreed, was the financial cost of accommodations. One national study estimated it would cost colleges $561 million to make changes that would allow students in wheelchairs to attend. The cost was formidable, Redden agreed, but well worth it. "[W]e are talking about a person's life and opportunities and I don't think this country can say it isn't worth spending the money," she said.

COURT GAINS AND SETBACKS

In several subsequent Supreme Court decisions, justices ruled against plaintiffs with disabilities, but they also upheld the validity of antidiscrimination bans. The Court rejected the demand of patients with disabilities for better Medicaid coverage in the 1985 case *Alexander* v. *Choate*. But the Court's decision in the case recognized that discrimination against people with disabilities occurred most often as the result of "thoughtlessness and indifference" and that Congress intended that reasonable accommodations be made even when the discrimination was unintentional.

Disability activists used the 1984 case of *Consolidated Rail Corporation* v. *Darrone* to present their views on disability issues. The suit involved the case of Thomas LeStrange, a train engineer at Conrail who lost his left hand and forearm in 1971 as the result of an accident that occurred while he was not at work. After he recovered, he sought another job at the company, but Conrail refused to employ him. The engineer died in 1982, and his daughter, Lee Ann LeStrange Darrone, sued, claiming the company had discriminated against LeStrange because of his disability. Darrone sought to recover back pay LeStrange would have collected had he been employed. The U.S. Department of Justice and the Disability Rights Education and Defense Fund (DREDF) both submitted briefs in support of Darrone's claims.

In a unanimous decision, the Supreme Court ruled against the corporation and for Darrone. Delivered on February 28, 1984, the decision reaffirmed the rights of workers with disabilities under Section 504 of the Rehabilitation Act. The Court's ruling offered antidiscrimination protection to workers with disabilities at all federally funded companies, not just those hired as a result of a program financed by government money. To do otherwise, Justice Lewis F. Powell Jr. stated in his opinion, would inflict a "drastic limitation on the handicapped individual's right to sue." One of the Rehabilitation Act's purposes, Justice Powell noted, was to "promote and expand employment opportunities in the public and private sectors for handicapped individuals and to place such individuals in employment."

The justices came to the opposite conclusion in another case, *Grove City College* v. *Bell*. Delivered the same day as the Conrail decision, the ruling in the *Grove City College* case undermined disability rights and set back civil rights for other minorities. The court case revolved around Title IX of the Education Amendments to the Civil Rights Act, which barred discrimination against women at all schools receiving federal funds. In deciding the case, the Court ruled that only the student grant program, the one operation at the school to receive federal funds, had to meet antidiscriminatory regulations, not the entire college.

President Ronald Reagan used the *Grove City College* case to ease rules that banned discrimination against Americans with disabilities, minorities, and others. Under his policies, businesses and institutions that received federal funds no longer had to eliminate discriminatory practices company-wide. Only the specific programs receiving federal funds had to comply with antidiscriminatory rules. Reagan's policies were a major setback for Americans with disabilities who sought access to public buildings, jobs, transportation, and other arenas.

Advocates for disability rights scored a big victory with a 1987 Supreme Court decision that people with contagious diseases could be considered "handicapped" under Section 504 of the Rehabilitation Act. The case involved an elementary school teacher who was fired after suffering a third relapse of tuberculosis. In its ruling, the Court barred the school board from firing the teacher solely on the basis of her illness. Furthermore, the decision made it clear that school boards and others receiving federal funds could not discriminate against people because of fear or suspicion. In making the law, the decision noted, Congress realized that society's "myths and fears about disability and disease" were "as handicapping as . . . the actual impairment." Each case, the court ruled, would have to be evaluated to determine whether a person with a contagious disease posed an actual danger to others while on the job. People with AIDS would later rely on this decision to fight their own court battles against discrimination.

FIGHTING "REAGANOMICS"

During the 1980s advocates for disability rights waged a continual battle against the Reagan administration's attempts to gut the Rehabilitation Act. President Reagan named his vice president, George H. W. Bush, to head the Task Force on Regulatory Relief. The task force was charged with eliminating regulations that businesses found objectionable. Included in

200 Protesters, One Jail Cell

The movement for disability rights was loud, insistent, some-times rude, but almost always nonviolent. Most participants were law-abiding citizens who used persuasion and lobby-ing skills to change policy. Those involved in protests occa-sionally landed in jail briefly for disorderly conduct or other minor charges. Others used the law's own shortcomings to make their point.

That was the case in the mid–1980s when nearly two hun-dred people with disabilities marched, walked, and rolled to the Michigan state capitol in Lansing to demand access to public buses. The protesters, led by Leonard Sawisch and his group STIGMA (Students for Total Integration through Greater Mobility and Accessibility), had obtained a parade permit to ensure that the demonstration would be legal. When organizers went to the police department to apply for the permit, an officer suggested they take buses to the capitol rather than walk.

"We can't!" said Sawisch, a psychologist and disability rights activist who is a dwarf. "They're not accessible. That's what we're protesting."

The police officer then suggested that the demonstra-tors stay on the sidewalks for safety's sake. "Great," replied Sawisch, "but there aren't curb cuts."

So through the streets they went. At one point the gather-ing stopped to rest at an intersection, briefly preventing the city buses from continuing on their routes. The police threat-ened to arrest the demonstrators until Sawisch reminded the officers that the city had only one jail cell that was accessible to people in wheelchairs and it could hold only two at a time. No arrests were made, and the marchers continued peace-fully on to the capitol building.

these regulations were the ones enforcing Section 504 of the Rehabilitation Act.

In May 1982 Americans with disabilities packed a meeting called by the Reagan administration to review changes in programs and regulations affected by the new federalism. Opponents of the changes delivered petitions signed by well over 100,000 people, along with bags of postcards and letters all demanding that the antidiscrimination regulations remain intact. On the third day of the meeting, held in Washington, D.C., Kathryn McInnis and Tom Andrews, executive director of the Maine Association of Handicapped Persons (MAHP) who later became Maine's U.S. representative in Congress, led a walkout to protest the administration's plan to weaken the rules. Francis Lynch, an official in the Department of Health and Human Services, had just told the gathering that the federal government was not responsible for people's well-being, even those with disabilities. The responsibility, he said, lay with the person first, the family second, and the community third. At that point, Andrews, who had lost a leg to cancer as a young man, shouted, "Our rights, our dignity, our quality of life are being sacrificed here." Another member of the audience cried, "Walk out or crawl out or roll out!" Most of the 150 people attending the meeting—many on crutches or in wheelchairs—left in protest.

For two years disability rights activists kept the pressure on the Reagan administration and on Congress. Thousands wrote letters, spoke at hearings, and contacted their members of Congress to protest any attempt to deregulate Section 504. MAHP organized a caravan that traveled along the entire East Coast and collected more than 68,000 postcards and letters protesting the move to weaken the law. In 1982 C. Boyden Gray, chief counsel to Vice President Bush, held hearings attended by thousands of people with disabilities and parents of children with disabilities. They spoke of the disastrous effect Reagan's proposals would have on their lives. Members of Congress from both political parties also urged the administration not to alter the 504 regulations or cut funding to enforce them. Finally, under pressure, Reagan and Bush abandoned the effort in 1983. Bush announced in a letter to Evan Kemp Jr. of the Washington-based Disability Rights Center that the regulations would not be changed. The vice president wrote that the administration shared Kemp's "commitment to equal opportunity for disabled citizens to achieve their full potential as independent, productive citizens." The episode helped educate Bush and Gray about disability issues. It also forged a bond between Bush and Kemp, who was later appointed to chair the Equal Employment Opportunity Commission (EEOC) by Bush, when he became president. Kemp became an important ally in the effort to pass the ADA.

The success of the campaign to protect Section 504 from deregulation galvanized the entire movement. Even Reagan's Republican Party realized the strength of the movement's lobby. During Reagan's reelection campaign, the Republicans included in their 1984 platform a section devoted to people with disabilities. It stated that "developing the individual dignity and potential of disabled Americans is an urgent responsibility. To these ends, the Republican Party commits itself to prompt and vigorous enforcement of the rights of disabled citizens."

BUS RIDE TO FREEDOM

Like the civil rights campaign waged by black Americans in the 1960s, the first big battle over rights for people with

Evan Kemp Jr., left, of the Disability Rights Center, meets with Vice President George H. W. Bush in 1983. Kemp played a pivotal role in stopping the Reagan administration from weakening existing disability laws.

disabilities revolved around public buses. In this case, how-ever, riders with disabilities were not relegated to the back of the bus; they were prevented from riding the buses alto-gether. While the Rehabilitation Act of 1973 barred dis-crimination on job sites supported by federal funds, many would-be employees had no way of getting to work—or anywhere else, for that matter. In communities across the nation, activists began pushing for accessible transportation for people with disabilities, framing it not as a subsidized service but as a civil right.

In November 1981 the Maine Association of Handicapped Persons invited the diverse branches of the movement to come together at a civil rights conference in Augusta, the state capital. The conference attracted veterans with disabilities, blind and deaf people, people in wheelchairs and with other mobility limitations, parents of children with disabilities, and others in the region. "Before, people had been pitted against each other for federal programs and benefits," said Kathryn McInnis, then on MAHP's board of directors. "This was the first time they had all been together."

More than five hundred people attended the conference. At the civic center, where it was held, organizers had equipped bathrooms with temporary grab bars and curtains to accommodate people in wheelchairs. An interpreter communicated MAHP's message to those with hearing difficulties. People with different disabilities face different challenges, and those attending the conference left with a better understanding of one another's concerns. The resulting plan of action focused on issues that would enable people to become independent: jobs, transportation, health care, and education. City buses, inaccessible to many people with disabilities, were chosen as the group's first target.

MAHP took on the federal government and local transit authorities to gain access to public transportation for people with disabilities. In March 1983 MAHP sued the city of South Portland in state court to force the city to equip its public buses with lifts to make them accessible to wheelchairs. The case became the first in the nation in which a court ruled that access to public transportation was a civil right. MAHP based its case on the Maine Human Rights Act, passed in 1971, which required "equal access to places of public accommodation" for people with disabilities. Under the state law, such access was recognized as a civil right. The focus on civil rights represented a dramatic shift in the way people with disabilities were viewed—not as dependents in need of subsidies but as citizens demanding equal rights.

The city of South Portland, like many others, ran a federally funded program that provided transportation to people with disabilities. The city contended that the program met the requirements of the Maine Human Rights Act by providing access to transportation to people with disabilities. The specially equipped vans, however, could be used only to ride to medical appointments. People in wheelchairs had to find their own way to grocery stores, jobs, clothing shops, movies, sports events, and other activities. Visiting friends was often impossible. Those who needed to use the vans had to make reservations, sometimes days in advance, to get a ride. Vans were frequently in the repair shop or had faulty lifts, causing would-be riders to miss medical appointments.

On August 13, 1984, the Maine Superior Court ruled in favor of MAHP. Echoing the words of the U.S. Supreme Court in the 1954 landmark case, *Brown v. Board of Education*, that ended school segregation, Justice Donald Alexander of the Maine Superior Court ruled that the transportation provided to riders with disabilities in South Portland was "both separate from and unequal to" the bus service others enjoyed. Under the ruling, the city had sixty days to devise a plan that would allow riders with disabilities to use the public bus system. The court cited the state's Human Rights Act in its decision. "Because public accommodations accessibility is a civil right," Alexander ruled, "there may not be separation or discrimination in the manner that the service is provided if reasonable accommodation . . . can be accorded."

The city of South Portland appealed the superior court ruling, and in April 1986 the Maine Supreme Court upheld the lower court's decision. The ruling required that all Maine municipalities equip buses with lifts. By then, many cities in the United States had wheelchair lifts on new buses.

On July 6, 1987, McInnis rode to the mall in one of the first buses to be equipped with a lift. Shopping for food at a grocery store with a friend, she began to cry. She had not realized until then what a sense of freedom the bus provided. "My life no longer required two weeks or 72 hours to schedule. I could catch a bus every half hour," she said later. "That was too cool."

"SEPARATE IS NEVER EQUAL"

News of the victory spread throughout the disability community. The court decision, said MAHP director Andrews, "impacts state human rights acts nationwide." Encouraged by the Maine group's success, other Americans with disabilities began demanding their civil rights around the country. In the fall of 1987 more than two hundred protesters marched to Connecticut's capitol demanding that the state adopt policies making public transportation more accessible. The demonstration was organized by Citizens for Accessible Transportation, a coalition of twenty Connecticut disability rights groups.

MAHP also sued the Reagan administration to force the government to issue regulations on the right of people with disabilities to use public transportation. The rules issued as part of the Rehabilitation Act of 1973 required public bus systems using federal funds to buy only buses with lifts until half the buses they operated at peak times were wheelchair-accessible. After the American Public Transit Association sued over the regulations in 1979, the court of appeals in Washington, D.C., ruled that the requirements were too severe and that "modest, affirmative steps to accommodate

Making a Difference

One day several years after the South Portland bus victory, Kathryn McInnis boarded a bus downtown. By that time all the bus drivers knew her well. The smiling driver indicated a young boy of nine or ten, seated in his wheelchair on the bus.

"This young man was just talking about one of his heroes," the driver told McInnis. Trying to guess the youngster's idol, McInnis named several sports heroes, then celebrities who typically appeal to young boys. To each name, the boy shook his head. Out of ideas, McInnis asked him to tell her the name of the person he admired.

"Kathy McInnis," he said, beaming. "Do you know her? If you don't, you should read about her. She's the reason for the buses, and now I don't have to have my mom push me to school."

McInnis, beaming herself, said she knew his hero very well. After a long look, the boy's mother realized who she was. Amid tears and smiles, they chatted for the rest of the trip. The boy's mother told McInnis later that teaching her son about the disability movement's heroes had helped him accept his own disability. "It was the only thing I could think of," she said, "to make him stop hating himself."

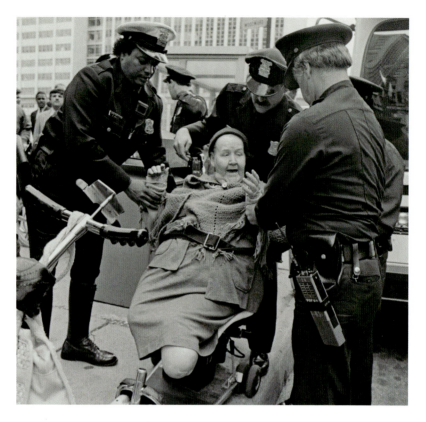

Edith Harris of Hartford, Connecticut, is arrested for blocking a Detroit bus in 1986. Harris was part of a group called American Disabled for Accessible Public Transit. Actions by such groups helped win support for regulations requiring public buses to be accessible to those in wheelchairs.

handicapped persons" would satisfy the law. The new regulations issued by the Department of Transportation (DOT) included a "local option" that allowed municipalities to provide separate transit systems for people with disabilities rather than equip public buses with lifts. In 1982 Congress passed the Surface Transportation Assistance Act, which directed the Department of Transportation to set up rules establishing "minimum criteria for the provision of transportation services to handicapped and elderly individuals."

When the Reagan administration failed to issue the new rules, MAHP filed suit. A federal district court judge in Maine ordered DOT to produce the required regulations.

When the department finally issued the rules, they allowed transit systems to spend no more than 3 percent of their annual budgets to make buses accessible. Other disability rights groups joined MAHP in another suit over the matter, among them American Disabled for Accessible Public Transit (ADAPT), founded in 1983. ADAPT would later play a leading role in organizing local activists for the ADA. After passage of the ADA, ADAPT changed its name to American Disabled for Attendant Programs Today and focused on helping people with disabilities live outside institutions.

In February 1989 a federal appeals court panel of three judges ruled that new buses purchased with federal money had to be accessible to riders with disabilities. A system that provided only special vehicles for riders with disabilities did not meet the requirements of Congress, the ruling declared. The court also struck down DOT's 3 percent limit. Writing for the panel, Judge Carol Los Mansmann noted, "Congress wanted to provide the disabled with the capability to utilize mass transit to the 'maximum extent feasible.'" The lawyer who argued the case for the coalition, Timothy M. Cook, called it a "major, major victory" for people with disabilities.

The government's decision to appeal the ruling sparked protests in more than a dozen cities, including New York City, San Francisco, and Washington, D.C. Protesters wearing signs reading SEPARATE IS NEVER EQUAL traveled through city streets on crutches, with canes, and in wheelchairs.

On July 24, 1989, the full court of appeals issued a mixed ruling. In a setback for the coalition, the decision allowed transit systems to avoid equipping public buses with wheelchair lifts if they ran an acceptable alternative system of specially equipped vehicles for passengers with disabilities. Lacking a "clear congressional mandate" requiring bus systems to give people with disabilities the same service as other riders, the court left the decision to DOT. Judge Mansmann disagreed, but she was in the minority. "Only a mixed-system of lift-equipped buses for those able to utilize them and a paratransit system for those who cannot will adequately implement the statutory mandates," Mansmann declared in her opinion on the matter.

The second part of the court's decision agreed with the coalition's position that the 3 percent spending limit should be eliminated. While Congress did allow DOT to consider costs, the opinion noted, applying the limit meant that cities with fewer than one million people would never be able to provide adequate transportation service to those with disabilities. The court ordered DOT to come up with alternative regulations that would accomplish the law's goal.

The ruling spurred members of the disability rights movement to work harder to get the "clear congressional mandate" the court required. The ongoing effort would soon pay off in the enactment of the Americans with Disabilities Act.

FORMING A COALITION

In 1979 Mary Lou Breslin and others founded the Disability Rights Education and Defense Fund (DREDF) to protect the rights of people with disabilities. That year DREDF sponsored a conference in San Francisco attended by civil rights activists and advocates for disability rights. The event helped to cement the relationship between these two groups. Among the participants was the Leadership Conference on Civil Rights (LCCR), headed by lawyer Ralph Neas. The LCCR had

Pat Wright of the Disability Rights Education and Defense Fund, left, discusses upcoming legislation with Democratic Senator Tom Harkin of Iowa. Wright's work on the Americans with Disabilities bill was critical to its passage.

played a leading role in the passage of many civil rights bills. The organization's expertise in civil rights legislation would contribute to the ADA's ultimate success.

Pat Wright, who served as DREDF's director, was known as the "general" for her skill in marshaling the forces and negotiating tough decisions. Senator Tom Harkin, Democrat of Iowa, would later refer to her on the Senate floor as "the most effective advocate I have ever met." As a young woman, she had studied medicine but began working with people with disabilities after she became legally blind as the result of an eye disease. Wright noted that disability would affect everyone sometime in life. To her and others in the disability rights community, those without disabilities were TABs, or the "temporarily able-bodied."

The coalition of civil and disability rights groups celebrated its first success when Congress approved an extension of the Voting Rights Act of 1965. The extension required municipalities to make polling places accessible to elderly voters and those with disabilities. The bill, introduced in the House in 1983 by Representative Hamilton Fish Jr., Republican of New York, garnered support from 179 cosponsoring representatives. Senator David Durenberger, Republican from Minnesota, introduced a similar bill in the Senate. The legislation, known as the Voting Accessibility for the Elderly and Handicapped Act of 1984, became law on September 28, 1984. Neas, a key player in the effort, later said the victory was a major step forward in the battle for civil rights for people with disabilities. "If we had not won on the Voting Rights extension," he said, "I don't think we would have won any civil rights bills after."

LIVING AND WORKING INDEPENDENTLY

On another front, activists for disability rights were calling for programs that would allow more people with disabilities to live independently rather than in group homes and institutions. The National Council on Independent Living (NCIL), founded in 1982 to promote noninstitutional living and disability rights, concentrated its efforts on setting up independent-living centers. Until the 1970s most programs were designed to rehabilitate those with disabilities to allow them to live and work without special adaptations. Those who could not function without modifications were cared for in institutions or homes apart from the rest of society.

Beginning in the 1970s people with disabilities began to push for modifications to make it possible for them to become active members of society. Like black Americans and women before them, people with disabilities rejected the stereotype that labeled them as inferior. Instead, they insisted that society open its doors to them. One of the first facilities to help people with disabilities live on their own, the Berkeley Center for Independent Living, opened its doors in 1972. The center, founded by a group of Berkeley students with disabilities, offered counseling; referrals for competent aides, jobs, and housing; and wheelchair repairs and modifications to vehicles to make them easier for drivers with disabilities to control. It also served as a model for centers set up in other cities and a hub of political activism to promote disability rights.

Rights advocates also set out to change the public view of people with disabilities as damaged, pathetic, and helpless beings who needed to be taken care of and who depended on donations and government funds to survive. Evan Kemp Jr. led the crusade against telethons like the one aired by the Jerry Lewis Muscular Dystrophy Association, which portrayed people with disabilities as sick children waiting for a cure. Kemp, who had a degenerative muscle disorder and used a wheelchair to get around, had served as a government lawyer before becoming director of the Disability Rights Center. Many people with disabilities believed that generating pity to raise money undercut their efforts to show the public that people with disabilities could earn a living and function in society. "An incredible amount of paternalism has always greeted the handicapped," said Leslie Milk, executive director of Mainstream, an organization providing support for people with disabilities to live in society. "People say, we will protect you from yourself, stay on the first floor of the world and you'll be safe. We're saying that we have the right to take risks."

CIVIL RIGHTS RESTORATION ACT

Shortly after the 1984 Supreme Court ruling in the *Grove City College* case, the rights coalition urged Congress to pass a bill to counteract the effects of the decision. Under the proposed Civil Rights Restoration Act, introduced by sympathetic members of Congress, recipients of federal funds would be required to ban discrimination throughout their institutions, not just in the specific programs receiving the federal money. Reagan and his Republican supporters in the Senate blocked the bill through a series of delay tactics. Opponents tacked on 1,300 amendments to the legislation before the final vote to kill the measure.

Senator Edward M. Kennedy, Democrat from Massachusetts, one of the chief sponsors of the bill, castigated the Senate for its action. "Shame on the Senate," he said. "We are being asked to sweep under the rug a basic and fundamental issue: whether Federal taxpayers funds should be used by programs that discriminate against the handicapped, minorities and the aged."

The civil rights and disability rights coalition continued the fight for the Civil Rights Restoration Act in the next Congress. Each group brought its own network of supporters to the campaign. The partnership eventually overwhelmed the opposition. On March 22, 1988, Congress passed the bill, which reversed the effects of the *Grove City College* ruling and reinstated the ban against discrimination in entire institutions that received federal funding for any of their programs. Reagan, who claimed the bill would burden institutions and businesses with new regulations, vetoed it. However, a strong coalition of Democrats and Republicans voted to override the veto, passing the bill with a 292 to 133 vote in the House and a 73 to 24 vote in the Senate. A contingent of people with disabilities cheered the final vote from a packed Senate gallery.

"People who voluntarily take Federal funds have an obligation to treat everybody else fairly," Representative Barney Frank, Democrat of Massachusetts, said after the vote. Republican senator Lowell P. Weicker Jr. of Connecticut, one of the main sponsors of the bill, noted that people with mental illnesses had once been "relegated by our prejudices to the darkness of despair" and black Americans had been "servants in their own country." The new law was designed to end that kind of discriminatory treatment of minorities, including those with disabilities.

The battle over the bill forged a lasting partnership between civil rights and disability rights advocates. It helped frame the fight for access as a civil rights issue, which activists would use later in pushing for a civil rights bill for people with disabilities. It also confirmed that such a bill was necessary. With the weakening of federal funding requirements and the Reagan administration's reluctance to enforce anti-discrimination laws, disability activists resolved to put all their energy into winning the fight for civil rights.

The coalition won another victory later that year with the passage of the Fair Housing Amendments Act, enacted on September 13, 1988. That bill added people with disabilities, including those with AIDS and mental illnesses, to the list of groups protected against discrimination when buying or renting housing. In addition, the law required that new multifamily buildings be accessible to renters in wheelchairs, with bathrooms that could be equipped with grab bars and other features for those with disabilities. Under the law, responsibility for filing suit against landlords accused of discriminatory housing practices shifted from individuals to the Department of Housing and Urban Development (HUD). In the past HUD merely served as a mediator in discrimination cases involving housing. "Until now, the Federal Fair Housing Act has represented little more than a policy statement," said Wade Henderson of the American Civil Liberties Union. "The aggrieved parties had to make their case, even though they usually lacked the resources to do so." For the first time, a law barred private businesses—not just those receiving federal funds—from discriminating against people with disabilities.

Regulations for the Air Carrier Access Act issued in 1990 barred airlines from charging people with disabilities extra fees or not allowing them to board planes altogether.

These successes demonstrated the effectiveness and skill of the disabilities rights lobby and helped pave the way for the ADA. Arlene Mayerson, lawyer and legal strategist for DREDF, noted that during these legislative campaigns, disability activists developed "working relationships with members of Congress and officials of the administration that proved indispensable in passing the ADA."

CHAPTER FIVE

The Evolution of a Law

During each two-year session of Congress, members introduce ten thousand bills or more. Only a small percentage of those are debated; the number of bills enacted is smaller still, about 6 percent. It takes tremendous effort to persuade Congress to treat a particular bill seriously enough to debate it, and then another huge campaign to win passage in a form that resembles the original intent of the legislation. Each of Congress's two branches, the House of Representatives and the Senate, has an opportunity to revise, amend, add, and subtract sections of the bill.

COMPREHENSIVE LAW NEEDED

The writing of the Americans with Disabilities Act began with the work of the National Council on the Handicapped, later renamed the National Council on Disability (NCD). Formed in 1978 to ensure equal opportunities to Americans with disabilities, the council initially operated under the direction of the U.S. Department of Health, Education, and Welfare. As part of its duties the council issued periodic reports on the status of people with disabilities.

To gather information for a report on disabilities, Justin Dart Jr., whom President Reagan had appointed as a vice-chair of the council, and his wife, Yoshiko, set out on a nation-wide tour, paying the expenses themselves. From October 1982 to August 1983 the council held public forums in every state and recorded the stories of people with disabilities who told of the discrimination they faced in jobs, housing, education, transportation, and other areas of their lives. These personal accounts were incorporated into the council's 1983 report. The document, published in August 1983, called for a national policy regarding people with disabilities that would allow them equal opportunities and laws that would protect them from discrimination.

While the Reagan administration supported "equal opportunity" that would allow people to work instead of collecting federal subsidies, the conservative Republican president balked at requiring private businesses to make accommodations for people with disabilities. Fearing that Reagan would disband the council or bury its work, Congress set it up as an independent agency in 1984. Congress then ordered the council to examine federal laws and programs that affected people with disabilities and to make recommendations on changes that should be made.

Once again the Darts conducted public forums throughout the United States. The council's resulting report, "Toward Independence," contained forty-five proposals to reduce the barriers to jobs, housing, transportation, education, and other services that Americans with disabilities faced every day. The council's first recommendation called for passage of a comprehensive federal law "requiring equal opportunity for individuals with disabilities, with broad coverage and setting clear, consistent, and enforceable standards prohibiting discrimination on the basis of handicap." Existing laws on disability, while offering some help, did not provide the broad prohibition against discrimination that civil rights laws protecting other groups did, according to the report. The proposed law would outlaw discrimination based on disability in all areas, not just those with ties to federal funding.

"If the goals of independence and access to opportunities for people with disabilities are to be achieved," the report stated, "it is essential that unfair and unnecessary barriers and discrimination not be allowed to block the way." The Americans with Disabilities Act would be the first step toward achieving those goals, the council declared.

By February 1987 Robert Burgdorf, a lawyer and staff member of the NCD, had completed the first draft of the ADA. For the next nine months the council reviewed the draft and worked with people with disabilities throughout the country to fine-tune it.

When the NCD issued its follow-up report to Congress in January 1988, it included a draft of the Americans with Disabilities Act. The report and the work of the disability coalition attracted attention and support from an impressive array of politicians. Senator Lowell P. Weicker Jr. agreed to sponsor the bill in the Senate. Representative Tony Coelho, the Democratic majority whip from California, vowed to do the same in the House. In August 1988 Vice President George H. W. Bush, the Republican Party's candidate for president, pledged to support the bill. His Democratic opponent in the race for the presidency, Massachusetts governor Michael Dukakis, endorsed disability rights, as did Senator

Justin Dart Jr.,

For more than five decades Justin Dart Jr. led the international campaign for rights for people with disabilities. Dart, the grandson of the founder of Walgreens drugstores, was born in Chicago in 1930 and contracted polio when he was eighteen. He later said "the good days" of his life began with the illness that left him in a wheelchair.

After more than a year in a rehabilitation center, Dart went to college, earned a master's degree from the University of Houston, and attended the University of Texas law school. When college officials refused to certify him as a high school teacher because of his disability, Dart went to work in Japan for the family business. While in Japan, he met and later married Yoshiko Saji, an executive at the Tupperware firm, owned by the Dart conglomerate. She would also become his partner in all of the many campaigns for disability rights.

On his return to the United States in the mid–1970s, Dart wrote extensively about hiring workers with disabilities. His work on the Governor's Committee on Disabilities in Texas brought him national attention, and in 1981 President Ronald Reagan named Dart to serve on the National Council on the Handicapped. In 1983 the council developed a national policy on disability rights, outlined in a report that Dart helped write.

As a member of the council and later as chair of the Congressional Task Force on the Rights and Empowerment of Americans with Disabilities, Dart conducted and helped finance public forums across the nation, attended by thousands of people with disabilities. Their stories—of the barriers they faced in employment, housing, transportation, education, and other areas of their lives—became a key factor in winning public support and congressional votes for the Americans with Disabilities Act. During these hearings Dart kept a list of every participant and his or her contact information, a valuable resource that disability rights activists used to marshal support for the ADA.

ADA's Godfather

Disability rights activist Justin Dart Jr. speaks at the Democratic National Convention in Chicago in 1996. Dart, who contracted polio as a teenager, has been called the "Godfather of the ADA" for his work on behalf of the legislation and for the rights of people with disabilities.

A flamboyant figure who appeared at hearings wearing a cowboy hat and boots, Dart, accompanied by his wife, traveled throughout the country in his campaign for the ADA and disability rights. He chaired the President's Committee on the Employment of People with Disabilities and in 1995 helped found Justice for All, a nonprofit group dedicated to disability rights issues. In 1998 President Bill Clinton presented him with the Presidential Medal of Freedom, the highest honor awarded to civilians, for his work on behalf of the ADA. "Justin Dart literally opened the doors of opportunities to millions of our citizens by securing passage of one of the nation's landmark civil rights laws: The Americans With Disabilities Act," President Clinton told the gathering. "I don't know that I've ever known a braver person." As he left the stage, Dart took the medal from his own neck and placed it around his wife's in tribute to her contributions to the cause.

Kennedy. Many of the bill's most fervent supporters had firsthand experience with disabilities. Coelho had been diagnosed with epilepsy as a young man; Weicker's son had Down syndrome. Kennedy's sister Rosemary was developmentally disabled and his son Edward Jr. lost a leg to bone cancer at the age of twelve. Republican senator Bob Dole of Kansas, who had lost the use of his right arm and suffered other injuries in World War II, became a passionate advocate for the bill. Senator Tom Harkin, who had a deaf brother and a quadriplegic nephew, helped usher the bill through Congress. Senator Orrin Hatch, Republican from Utah, dedicated his work on the bill to his brother-in-law, who could not walk as a result of polio.

FRONT-PAGE NEWS

In March 1988 the topic of disability rights made front-page headlines around the world when deaf students and faculty at Gallaudet University in Washington, D.C., shut down the school to protest the trustees' selection of a non-deaf president. Established in 1864, the university served as the nation's only liberal arts college for people with hearing impairments. The protest put the spotlight on the rights of people with disabilities and won the support of several members of Congress and both presidential candidates. As a result, the university named Dr. I. King Jordan as its first deaf president and replaced the head of the trustees with a business executive from New York who was deaf. Senator Tom Harkin presented part of his comments in sign language at Jordan's installation later that year.

The protest and victory at Gallaudet meshed with the efforts being undertaken by other groups to pass civil rights legislation that would benefit all people with disabilities.

Deaf students at Gallaudet University in Washington, D.C., take part in a 1988 protest against the school's decision to hire a president who was not deaf. The protest shut down the university and succeeded in convincing the board to hire Dr. I. King Jordan as Gallaudet's first deaf president.

Rather than being organized under the direction of one central organization, however, the movement gathered strength from several sources. The Consortium for Citizens with Disabilities (CCD) united many organizations working for people with disabilities. The CCD's task force on civil rights focused its efforts on the enactment of a civil rights bill for those with disabilities. Chaired by Pat Wright of the Disability Rights Education and Defense Fund (DREDF), Liz Savage of the Epilepsy Foundation of America (EFA), and Curt Decker of the National Association of Protection and Advocacy Systems (NAPAS), the civil rights task force, worked with other coalitions and activists to win Congress's support for the bill.

ADAPT and the National Council on Independent Living (NCIL) were among the many organizations that undertook a state-by-state initiative to publicize the campaign, educate and win support from members of Congress, and galvanize supporters. The movement gained momentum from grassroots activists who worked for disability rights throughout the nation. Each success story highlighted the abilities of people with disabilities and their unwillingness to remain segregated or be denied a shot at the American dream. Activists also experienced firsthand the strength in numbers. Students with disabilities at Wright State University in Ohio, for example, persuaded officials to set up a sports program for them. "If it had been one person against [the] system, that never would have happened," said Roland Sykes, one of the student leaders who later created a computer network that linked disability rights activists. Kathryn McInnis recalled that advocates in Maine met with that state's congressional delegation many times to stress the need for a bill to protect disability rights. "I don't think we left them [the delegation] alone any time they were in Maine," she said.

INTRODUCING THE ADA

On April 28 and 29, 1988, Senator Lowell Weicker and Representative Tony Coelho introduced the Americans with Disabilities Act in the 100th Congress. With cosponsors from both parties in the Senate and the House, the ADA was truly a bipartisan effort. In proposing the legislation, Weicker told his colleagues in the Senate, "It is high time that we as a society formally and forcefully prohibit the discrimination that is the greatest handicap to Americans with disabilities." Noting that discrimination against people with disabilities was "substantial and pervasive," Senator Harkin, chair of the Senate Subcommittee on the Handicapped, urged Congress to support the bill.

The following week Congress formed a task force to gather examples of discrimination against Americans with disabilities and to make recommendations on how to correct the situation. Justin Dart Jr., named to head the task force, set out on another tour to collect people's own stories of discrimination. Over the next two years the task force held sixty-three public forums in every state in the nation. More than seven thousand attended, including people with all types of disabilities, parents and families of children with disabilities, teachers and health-care workers, and other advocates for those with disabilities. Thousands signed petitions supporting the ADA and wrote about their experiences with discrimination in accompanying documents. Dart and other members of the task force met with Congress, issued reports on their findings, and spoke with various organizations throughout the country on behalf of the ADA. They all worked without pay, and Dart and his wife, Yoshiko, personally attended many of the forums and footed the bill for much of the cost involved.

In September and October 1988 Senate and House subcommittees held hearings on disability rights. Hundreds of people with disabilities poured into Washington, D.C., to testify. Their personal stories gave members of Congress and the American public an insight into what it was like to live with a disability and to be discriminated against because of it. Judith Heumann was among the many whose powerful testimony touched listeners. Heumann, who had organized the San Francisco sit-in in the 1970s and was a leader in the disability rights campaign, testified that she had been barred from school at age five and told she was a fire hazard because she relied on a wheelchair as a result of polio. Another woman, Belinda Mason, described her life after being diagnosed with HIV, the virus that causes AIDS, from a blood transfusion. A neighbor circulated a petition to force her to move from town, and officials closed the municipal pool for a week after she swam there. Others told of being turned away at the polls, prevented from opening bank accounts, denied high school and college diplomas, and ignored by sales clerks, medical providers, and receptionists. The hearings, televised on C-Span, the public-affairs cable TV channel, reinforced the need for a disability rights law.

NEW CONGRESS, NEW STRATEGY

As the November election loomed, it became clear that the 100th Congress would take no final action on the ADA. Nevertheless, ADA proponents considered their efforts well spent as they laid the groundwork for the law's passage in the next Congress. Election 1988 brought mixed results. George H. W. Bush, who had pledged support for the ADA, won the presidency. Since the days he and Gray had worked with disability rights proponents on the Rehabilitation Act regulations, Bush had developed a respect for people with disabilities and an understanding of their needs. Those pushing for the ADA had a good working relationship with him, and advocates hoped the new president would persuade other Republicans to support the bill. The bad news was the loss of ADA champion Senator Weicker, defeated by Democrat Joseph Lieberman in his bid for reelection.

Senator Harkin agreed to take over the job of pushing the

bill through the Senate in the new Congress. By doing so, Harkin, a first-term Democratic senator, would undoubtedly make enemies of business leaders and local officials in his home state who opposed additional federal regulations on industry. Such opposition from the business lobby could put him at risk of losing his Senate seat in the next election. The senator, however, had no qualms in accepting the challenge. "I didn't get elected to get re-elected," he said. "My brother is deaf. I understand discrimination. I understand what it means and what this country can look like in thirty years. We are doing this legislation."

With the seating of a new Congress and president, ADA supporters planned their strategy. To win the backing of powerful leaders in the Senate and the House, the ADA of 1988 would have to be revised. Senator Kennedy, a longtime civil rights advocate, joined Harkin in rewriting the bill. It was a difficult task that required meeting the demands of the disability coalition while easing the fears of private businesses and government leaders.

A coalition of people with disabilities and their supporters across the country became the true authors of the Americans with Disabilities Act. Senate staff members headed by Robert Silverstein, staff director and chief counsel for the Subcommittee on the Handicapped, worked on the revisions with a formidable team of legal experts and strategists skilled in disability issues. These included Pat Wright and Arlene Mayerson of DREDF, Ralph Neas of LCCR, NCD's Robert Burgdorf, and Timothy Cook, executive director of the National Disability Action Center. They reviewed hundreds of national, state, and local laws on disability and civil rights issues. Leaders in the disability community nationwide, including Maine activist Kathryn McInnis, picked out passages they liked,

Senator Edward M. Kennedy, one of the leading proponents in the fight for passage of the ADA, poses with disability rights activists at the 1990 signing of the legislation. At far left are Tom Andrews of Maine and Kathryn McInnis (partially obscured).

suggested new provisions, and threw out ones that did not apply. These changes were then incorporated in new drafts to be reviewed by the legal team. The law group also consulted with congressmen, members of the administration, business leaders, and others who would be affected by a new law.

In preparing a bill designed to win support from Congress, the coalition nevertheless made a commitment not to exclude any group within the disability community. That decision held firm, even under extreme pressure from members of Congress not to cover people with mental illnesses or AIDS.

The finished bill focused on jobs, public services including transportation and education, public accommodations, and telecommunications. Modeled on the Civil Rights Act of 1964, the revised bill borrowed heavily from the 1973 Rehabilitation Act, expanding its provisions and borrowing many of its definitions. The new bill banned discrimination in public and private arenas and required businesses to make "reasonable accommodations" for workers and customers with disabilities. It expanded the scope of the original bill to cover small retail stores, office buildings, and professional offices as well as hotels, restaurants, and other facilities used by the public.

COMPROMISES AND A UNITED FRONT

In rewriting the law, the authors agreed to compromises that some in the disability community found hard to swallow. But everyone recognized the importance of presenting a united front once the bill was before Congress. Even the most passionate activists acknowledged the economic cost to businesses and the community and the need to win support from business-oriented lawmakers. The original bill had called for all buildings to be accessible within five years; the revised version allowed owners of older facilities more time to make alterations. Business owners could postpone compliance with the regulations if the modifications created "undue hardship," defined as "unduly costly, extensive, substantial, disruptive" or requiring actions that would "fundamentally alter the nature" of the business. Under the original bill, businesses were exempt only if the modifications threatened to bankrupt the firm or if they "fundamentally changed" the nature of the business. When buildings could not be modified by taking "readily achievable" steps, other provisions had to be made for people with disabilities. For example, programs might be offered elsewhere in an accessible building or a ramp installed at a side door. Similarly, the law required new buses and new stations to be accessible but allowed companies more leeway in regard to existing facilities and vehicles.

The new law also narrowed the definition of disability to people with "a physical or mental impairment that substantially limits one or more of the major life activities." So, for example, a person who had difficulty walking, seeing, or getting dressed would qualify for the act's protections. In addition, the act covered people who had "a record" of such a disability or who were treated by others as disabled.

REVISED ADA PRESENTED TO CONGRESS

On May 9, 1989, in a joint action in the Senate and the House, Senators Harkin and David Durenberger, Republican from Minnesota, and Representatives Tony Coelho and Hamilton Fish Jr., Republican from New York, introduced the revised version of the Americans with Disabilities Act to the 101st Congress. Eighty-four representatives cosponsored the bill in the House; thirty-three joined in backing the legislation in the Senate. More than eighty-five disability organizations, the Leadership Conference on Civil Rights (which represented 185 civil rights groups), and a number of religious alliances endorsed the bill. Supporters planned to get the bill through the Senate first, then concentrate on passing it in the House.

In his introductory remarks on the ADA, Harkin called the bill "the most critical legislation affecting persons with disabilities ever considered by Congress." Quoting Justin Dart Jr., he said the bill was "a landmark statement of human rights, which will, at long last, keep the promise of 'liberty and justice for all' to the nation's last large oppressed minority." The act, Harkin said, sent a "clear and unequivocal message to people with disabilities that they are entitled to be treated with dignity and respect and to be judged as individuals on the basis of their abilities." The ADA also made it clear to employers, businesses, transportation companies, state and local governments, and others that discrimination against people with disabilities was illegal and would be punished with "the full force of Federal law." The ADA was needed, Harkin said, because other civil rights laws did not protect Americans with disabilities from discriminatory acts. Barriers such as stairs, nonaccessible buses, and telephones unusable by deaf people would be targeted by the law, the senator noted.

Coelho had similar lofty words for the bill when he introduced it in the House. "This historic piece of legislation will prohibit discrimination against America's largest minority, people with disabilities, in employment, transportation, public accommodations, and the activities of State and local government," Coelho said. He noted that a major goal of the act was to eliminate job discrimination. Two-thirds of Americans with disabilities were unemployed, he noted, and the number of families of people with disabilities earning less than $5,000 a year was almost triple the national average. Of those unemployed, two-thirds of Americans with disabilities of working age wanted jobs. "This overwhelming absence from the labor force of people with a strong desire to work is a tragic failure of the American dream and a waste of labor resources," Coelho said.

Most of the work on the bill would be done in Senate and House committees. Committee members review each bill before them, hold hearings when warranted, propose amendments, and negotiate compromises. A bill often undergoes a major rewrite at these meetings, called markup sessions, during which committee members fashion a bill into final form before voting on it and issuing a report to the full House or Senate. The other members of Congress rely heavily on the work of the committees to guide them in dealing with the hundreds of bills proposed each year. The full House or Senate can still make changes to a bill once it leaves committee, but generally Congress follows the committee's recommendations, especially if the members issue a unanimous report. If several committee members oppose the majority view, however, the bill may face further revisions when it comes before the full House or Senate for debate.

On the same day the ADA was introduced in Congress, the Senate sent the bill to the Labor and Human Resources Committee, chaired by Senator Kennedy, for review. Although Senator Hatch—ranking Republican on the committee—declined to sponsor the bill initially, he would later help win Republican support for its passage, as would Minority Leader Robert Dole. Coelho began the testimony before the Senate committee, detailing his own experiences as someone who had a disability (epilepsy) and who had overcome obstacles to achieve success. "We can be productive if you will give us that right, give us that opportunity," he said. "That is all we ask for, nothing more, but definitely nothing less."

When Congress finally passed the ADA, neither Coelho nor Weicker, the original backers of the bill, would cast their votes on the legislation. Shortly after his Senate testimony, Coelho became the focus of a congressional inquiry when investigators questioned investments he had made. He resigned on June 15, saying he did not want to subject his party to further controversy over ethics charges. That left Representative Steny Hoyer, Democrat from Maryland, with the task of guiding the legislation through the House.

FINANCIAL PROS AND CONS

As expected, the cost to businesses and the government proved to be the major sticking point of the ADA. Building owners objected to the cost of converting old buildings to make them accessible to people with disabilities. Employers were concerned over the cost and effort involved in refitting workplaces for workers and customers with disabilities. The bill's advocates argued that putting people with disabilities to work would provide businesses with a valuable labor force. Harkin addressed the concerns of businesses when he introduced the bill, claiming the costs had been "exaggerated." He cited several examples of low-cost modifications made by companies for their workers with disabilities.

James Brady, President Ronald Reagan's former press secretary who was paralyzed by a would-be assassin's bullet in 1981, furthered that argument in an article supporting the ADA published in the *New York Times.* Brady, an officer of the National Organization on Disability, became one of the bill's most ardent advocates. As a fiscal conservative, Brady argued that the bill would not only help people with disabilities but would also benefit the economy by allowing those with disabilities to work, be consumers, and get off welfare. He urged passage of the bill, which, he said, "would free hundreds of thousands of citizens who are virtually prisoners in their homes because of inaccessible transportation and public accommodations." No civil right, he noted, had ever been won without being protected by a law.

Backers of the bill claimed the modifications it required would save some of the $60 billion the federal government spent each year to support unemployed people with disabilities. With jobs, they noted, workers with disabilities would pay taxes instead of surviving on federal subsidies. Some businesses supported the law or took no stance against it. An official at DuPont said similar requirements for businesses using federal grants was "not burdensome at all." According to a survey conducted for the Department of Labor in 1982, many changes required for employees with disabilities—like offering flexible work schedules—would cost little or nothing. For companies facing a labor shortage, people with disabilities offered a welcome source of workers, even if some modifications were required. "We're going to do whatever we can to bring more people into the work force," an official of the American Hotel and Motel Association told reporters.

Many business groups, however, opposed the ADA. Chief among the opposition was the U.S. Chamber of Commerce and a coalition of businesses, the Disability Rights Working Group, formed to defeat the bill in Congress. They objected to being saddled with the cost of making buildings and other accommodations accessible. Building ramps, revamping bathrooms, widening doors, and other changes, business owners noted, would carry a high price tag. The chairman of Greyhound Lines told Congress that wheelchair lifts for new buses could cost the company $40 million a year.

INTENSE LOBBYING

To counter the business lobbyists, people with disabilities and their supporters poured into Washington to push for the bill. While Congress debated and negotiated the bill's terms, this army of activists, many with severe disabilities, from every walk of life—young and old, rich and middle class and poor, teachers, doctors, parents, workers, veterans, and college students—lived in hotels or with friends for "weeks and weeks and weeks," said McInnis, who traveled from Maine to participate in the lobbying effort. They formed teams and visited every member of Congress and every senator to explain their support for the bill. "We're the faces of this movement," they told whoever would listen. Some testified before Congress; others worked behind the scenes, organizing data, counting votes, making telephone calls, and doing a thousand necessary tasks. "There were a lot of sleepless nights and a lot of hard work," McInnis recalled.

Thousands worked on the campaign. They sent their stories of discrimination to Congress, flooded congressional offices with postcards and letters in support of the bill, wrote letters to editors at newspapers across the nation, and collected signatures on petitions calling for the bill's passage. "There were a million little heroes around the country," McInnis noted.

Spectators packed committee rooms during hearings. Interpreters signed the proceedings to deaf members of the audience; others followed the action from their wheelchairs.

President Bush formally gave his approval to the ADA in June when Attorney General Richard Thornburgh announced to the committee that the administration was pledging its "full support for comprehensive civil rights legislation for persons with disabilities." The attorney general said the administration would "work in good faith" to address criticisms and develop a compromise bill that would pass Congress. "We must end the anomaly of widely protecting women and minorities from discrimination while failing to provide parallel protection for people with disabilities," Thornburgh told senators. "Persons with disabilities are still too often shut out of the economic and social mainstream of American life."

REACHING A COMPROMISE

The Senate committee continued to work on the legislation throughout the spring and early summer of 1989. Negotiations over the bill stalled in July when the Bush administration shifted its stance and balked at the broad reach of the bill.

White House chief of staff John Sununu and Attorney General Thornburgh argued that small businesses should not have to bear the cost of making their facilities accessible, that violators should not have to pay damages to those who sued them if they were found not in compliance with the law, and that only hotels, restaurants, theaters, and similar types of public venues should be regulated by the bill. Supporters resisted the administration's efforts to tamper with the legislation. Senator Harkin objected to an administration version of the bill that would require some businesses but not others to make their buildings accessible. He quoted testimony from a disability rights spokesperson at the hearings to make his point: "It makes no sense for a law to say that people with disabilities cannot be discriminated against if they want to buy a pastrami sandwich at the local deli but that they can be discriminated against next door at the pharmacy where they need to fill a prescription."

When Republican conservatives threatened to block the bill by holding it in committee, Senator Robert Dole used his considerable influence as minority leader to prevent the move. "We would never [have] gotten it through if Bob Dole hadn't been supportive," Coelho said later. Dole worked to resolve the differences between the administration and the rights groups. After intense negotiations, both sides agreed to a compromise. The new version of the bill eliminated the clause that required violators to pay damages. Instead, the ADA would adhere to the rules set up in the Civil Rights Act of 1964. Violators under that act could face court fines and be forced to reimburse back pay and reinstate fired workers. They would not have to pay compensatory or punitive damages, even when violators purposely discriminated against someone. Compensatory damages cover actual damages done to the victim; punitive damages are assessed to punish the violator and discourage further violations.

In return, the administration officials accepted that the bill would apply to almost all businesses, big and small. ADA proponents agreed to a delay in enforcing the employment regulations. Businesses with at least twenty-five employees would have two years to comply with the law; smaller companies would get a four-year reprieve. In addition, workers who used illegal drugs would not be protected from firing or other measures. Other revisions exempted religious groups and private clubs from modifying buildings to make them accessible and allowed an eighteen-month delay in the regulations for other public facilities. Private bus systems were given up to five years to add lifts to their vehicles. "It was worth the trade-off because the concept was so important," said Senator Kennedy, who participated in the negotiations.

On August 2 President Bush, reassured by the compromise, reiterated his support for the ADA. His statement added weight to the growing list of those urging the bill's passage. Following the Bush endorsement, Senator Hatch, the leading Republican member of the Senate Labor and Human Resources Committee, announced that he had agreed to cosponsor the bill. The committee then voted unanimously to pass the measure as amended and sent it to the full Senate for debate.

SENATE VOTES ITS APPROVAL

While Congress took a summer recess, business groups carried their concerns about the bill to the media. While not opposing the bill outright, they lobbied for amendments that would modify some requirements and exempt them from others. A U.S. Chamber of Commerce lawyer told reporters that the ADA would cost telephone companies more than $250 million a year and bus companies $40 million to $80 million annually. The National Federation of Independent Business also protested the cost of ADA regulations to its small-business members. Industry critics predicted that the law would result in "a wave of lawsuits." A *Wall Street Journal* editorial called the bill "the lawyers' employment act," echoing Senator Jesse Helms's cynical name for the ADA, the "Lawyers' Relief Act." The ADA, according to the business newspaper, was "a swamp of imprecise language; it will mostly benefit lawyers who will cash in on the litigation that will force judges to, in effect, write the real law."

On September 7, 1989, a day after reconvening, the Senate turned its full attention to the bill. For the first time in Senate history, interpreters for the deaf signed the debate from the Senate floor. Critics attacked the bill on several fronts. Pro-business senators debated for hours in an unsuccessful attempt to ease requirements to make buildings accessible. Senator Orrin Hatch and Senator Bob Kerrey, Democrat from Nebraska, proposed a tax credit to aid businesses that made modifications on their buildings, but the Senate rejected the amendment as too costly for the federal government. A handful of conservative Republicans led by Senator Jesse Helms of North Carolina and Senator William Armstrong of Colorado objected to the inclusion of people with AIDS or mental illnesses in the act, but proponents held firm. To appease the conservatives, backers of the bill agreed to exclude those with gambling addictions and "pedophiles, transsexuals, voyeurs and kleptomaniacs."

After a lengthy discussion, the Senate approved an amendment by Senator Charles Grassley, Republican of Iowa, to require Congress as well as other entities to abide by the law. "If it's too burdensome for the U.S. Congress to live by this bill's command, then why is it less burdensome for anyone else?" Grassley demanded. Late that night, after a long day of debate and amid broad support from both parties, senators voted 76 to 8 to adopt the ADA.

BEFORE THE HOUSE

Passage of the ADA by the Senate had taken four months. The bill's journey through the House would take twice as long and would require all the skills, patience, and persuasion the disability coalition could muster.

The House assigned four subcommittees—Judiciary; Education and Labor; Energy and Commerce; and Public Works and Transportation—to review the ADA, hold hearings on the bill, and consider amendments before releasing it for a vote by the full House. A fifth entity, the Small Business Committee, would also hold hearings but would take no vote on the ADA. The first House hearings, held jointly by the Employment Opportunity and Select Education subcommittees (within the Education and Labor Committee), began in mid-July.

The critics who had attacked the bill in the Senate took aim at the House version. While supporting the ADA's goals, U.S. Chamber of Commerce lawyer Nancy Fulco assailed the bill's vague wording, the fees imposed on violators, and the lack of firm estimates of its costs. "A full cost analysis of this bill has not been done by anybody I know," she said. Other business groups complained that businesses should not be the only ones to bear the burden of making society accessible to people with disabilities; the federal government should share in the costs.

People with disabilities packed the House committee hearings just as they had those held by the Senate. Hundreds attended a hearing in Houston, Texas, held in August by the House Select Education Subcommittee, where they shared their personal stories of discrimination. Government officials and business leaders, including some bus company representatives, also testified in support of the ADA at the hearing. The testimony helped persuade Texas representative Steve Bartlett, the subcommittee's ranking Republican, to take an active role in the bill's passage.

The subcommittee held four hearings on the bill in 1989 and considered more than twenty amendments to the ADA. Ultimately the subcommittee adopted several changes designed mainly to help businesses comply with the law. Among them were proposals to limit lawsuits, to allow businesses to perform drug tests and fire drug users not seeking treatment, and to consider a firm's finances when determining whether making alterations would be an "undue hardship."

ADA WINS COMMITTEE'S APPROVAL

On November 14, 1989, the House Committee on Education and Labor became the first to approve the amended bill and refer it to the full House. The unanimous vote reflected the broad bipartisan support for the ADA and gave proponents hope that Congress would enact the bill shortly after returning from the Christmas break.

Deliberations dragged on through the winter and into the spring of 1990. Business groups continued to press for further revisions in the bill. They sought amendments that would provide tax credits to help pay for modifications, a limit to businesses' out-of-pocket expenses for modifications, clearer definitions, and a list of the disabilities covered by the ADA.

Advocates for the bill continued to emphasize its benefits to employers. "ADA will help provide for the United States a talented work force which we will need to compete in the new global economy," Representative Romano Mazzoli, a Kentucky Democrat, told his colleagues in the House on March 1. "It will facilitate the hiring and the employment of talented, productive men and women who happen to be impaired or handicapped in some fashion."

The most emotional debate concerned the attempt by conservatives to remove people with AIDS and HIV from the bill's protections. During deliberations by the Energy and Commerce Committee in March, Representative William Dannemeyer, a California Republican, introduced amendments designed to eliminate people with contagious or sexually transmitted diseases from the bill's protections. In defending his proposal, he said he wanted to exclude only "homosexuals or drug addicts" who had AIDS, not those who had contracted it through blood transfusions. The committee rejected Dannemeyer's amendments after a heated exchange.

Other passionate disputes took place in March and April when ADA critics targeted the inclusion in the bill of people with mental illnesses. The *Gazette Telegraph* in Colorado Springs published a cartoon portraying a crazed man wielding a chain saw at a terrified group of workers and a personnel manager, who complained that the ADA made him hire the man. The cartoon triggered a protest by forty people outside the newsroom. Using similar tactics, Representative Chuck Douglas, a New Hampshire Republican, circulated a letter to his colleagues on the Judiciary Committee that featured a drawing of a man aiming an assault rifle accompanied by a news clipping about a man with a mental illness who killed seven people. The legislator warned that the ADA would force employers to hire "dangerous people." The crude messages brought immediate protests from ADA proponents, advocates for people with mental illnesses, and other Americans outraged by what they regarded as bigotry and scare tactics. "It's like taking an article on child abuse and then saying all women are child abusers," protested Rona Purdy, president of the New Hampshire chapter of the Alliance for the Mentally Ill.

Much less controversial were provisions governing telecommunications for the deaf. The Energy and Commerce Committee beefed up a provision that required states to set up a relay system manned by an operator for deaf people who did not have access to a TDD (telecommunication device for the deaf). Under the system, a person who did not have access to a TDD but wanted to phone a deaf person could call the relay service. An operator would then relay the message to the deaf person using a TDD. The committee's amendment removed a loophole that made exceptions for states claiming an "undue burden." The committee also passed an amendment requiring that all public service announcements relying on federal funds have closed captions for the deaf.

TRANSPORTATION WOES

One of the biggest challenges to the bill's passage revolved around transportation. The Energy and Commerce Committee, which had jurisdiction over Amtrak passenger trains, took several months to come to a consensus on the issue. The committee eventually forged regulations for Amtrak, including the requirement that one car per train be accessible and that all new cars be built to accommodate wheelchairs. On March 13, 1990, the House Energy and Commerce Committee overwhelmingly approved the amended ADA by a 40 to 3 vote. Representative Hoyer called the vote "another giant leap toward floor consideration and enactment."

A group of people with disabilities gather outside the Capitol Building on March 12, 1990, in support of the Americans with Disabilities bill.

Transportation issues posed dilemmas for the Public Works and Transportation Committee as well. Greyhound warned that the extra costs required to put wheelchair lifts on its buses could outpace expected yearly profits and threaten the bus line's existence. Under those conditions, Greyhound would be forced to raise fares and eliminate less profitable rural routes, according to company officials. ADA proponents argued that because the bus line provided the only public transportation available in some rural communities, riders with disabilities would be stranded without wheelchair lifts. The committee decided to follow the Senate's recommendation that regulations be postponed until a study could be conducted on the situation.

Operators of commuter rail services sought their own modifications to the ADA. In March industry interests won a temporary victory when some Democrats joined Republicans on the committee and approved an amendment that would allow commuter rail companies to have only a certain number of cars per train accessible to riders with disabilities. The original bill required that all new cars be accessible, a regulation that industry officials claimed would cost millions of dollars. Sponsors of the amendment, Illinois Representatives William Lipinski, a Democrat, and Dennis Hastert, a Republican, insisted that the new provision would not injure the bill "in any way." Disappointed advocates for those with disabilities said the change could mean long waits for some riders with disabilities. On April 3, with the amendment in place, the Public Works and Transportation Committee voted 45 to 5 to approve the ADA. The amendment would later be replaced by the version from the Energy and Com merce Committee that required all new cars to be accessible.

NEW COMPLICATIONS

Only one committee, Judiciary, remained to act on the bill. That committee addressed the bill's effect on public accommodations and other matters. After three hearings, it appeared that the committee would readily approve the bill. Complications arose, however, when the Senate introduced a revision to the original Civil Rights Act that would allow violators to be sued for damages. Because the ADA was linked to the Civil Rights Act, the revision would also apply to the disability rights law. Representative James Sensenbrenner, Republican from Wisconsin, introduced an administration-backed amendment that would have eliminated ADA's link to the Civil Rights Act and prevented workers with disabilities from collecting damages. The majority of the committee rejected the amendment, which the disability rights coalition strongly opposed.

Disability rights activists were growing impatient over the long delay. On March 12 more than 250 people with disabilities gathered for a "Wheels of Justice" rally at the White House. The protesters, many in wheelchairs, moved to the steps leading up to the Capitol to urge Congress to pass the ADA. "We're here to send a message to the President and to Congress that this bill needs to be passed with no weakening amendments," said Bob Kafka, a quadriplegic activist from Austin, Texas.

On May 2, the Judiciary Committee voted 32 to 3 in favor of the ADA. On May 14 and 15 the four committees submitted their reports and ADA amendments to the Rules Committee. It would be up to that entity to review each committee's version of the ADA and fashion them into one bill. After more than a day of debate, the Rules Committee agreed to eight amendments that would be considered by the full House when debating the bill.

"AN AMERICAN MILESTONE"

On May 17 people with disabilities from around the nation gathered in the capital as the House of Representatives opened debate on the ADA. Those who could not get into the galleries above the House floor watched the proceedings on television sets in Statuary Hall, the chamber where the House conducted its business in the first half of the 1800s.

Representative Hoyer, who had orchestrated the bill's winding passage through the House committees and sub-committees, announced the arrival of the ADA on the floor. "It is a bill whose time is too late but whose time has certainly come," he told the waiting crowd. During the debate, proponents of the bill in Congress fought back most of the eight amendments that would have weakened the ADA's protections. Representative Sensenbrenner promoted the amendment to sever the link between the ADA and the Civil Rights Act. Despite the president's support of the amendment, the House voted against it, 227 to 192.

Another amendment required companies to pay no more than 10 percent of the salary of an employee with disabilities for modifications. The amendment, opposed by the disability coalition, was defeated by a 213 to 187 vote. The House also rejected an amendment that would have allowed commuter railroads to equip only one car per train for riders with disabilities instead of making all new cars accessible. An amendment proposed by Representative Bud Shuster, Republican from Pennsylvania, would have given small communities the option of providing special vans for riders with disabilities, instead of bus lifts. That, too, was defeated, 266 to 148.

One amendment that did get through on a close 199 to 187 vote allowed businesses to bar workers with "contagious diseases," including AIDS, from handling food and move them to other jobs. Public health officials stated that AIDS could not be transmitted through food, but proponents nevertheless sold the amendment as necessary to protect public health. The controversial amendment, promoted by Texas Democrat Jim Chapman and New Hampshire's Douglas, was a setback for the entire disability rights community, which had pledged to push for antidiscrimination protections for all Americans with disabilities. Floor leader Hoyer referred to the Chapman proposal as the "Jim Crow amendment of 1990" and predicted that the Senate would reject the measure during final conferences with the House on the ADA.

The House also approved two amendments that benefited business owners. One gave small companies extra time to meet the law's rules before they would be subject to civil suits. The second required courts to consider an employer's description of the tasks necessary to a job when judging whether a worker with a disability would be qualified. A final amendment, to allow wheelchairs in protected wilderness areas, passed without controversy.

On May 22, 1990, after months of testimony and negotiations, the House approved the ADA by a vote of 403 to 20. Banner headlines in newspapers around the nation proclaimed it "the most sweeping civil rights bill in two decades" and "an American milestone." Amid cheers and tears, McInnis witnessed the vote from her wheelchair in the House gallery. "If you're going to have civil rights for some people," she told a *USA Today* reporter, "you've got to have it for everyone."

TASTING FREEDOM

With the House vote, the ADA headed to conference, where House and Senate members would thrash out differences in the two versions of the bill. To the relief of ADA supporters, administration officials announced that the president would not veto the bill over the issue of workers' suing for damages, as some had feared.

As it became apparent that the bill would be enacted, people who had worked for so many years to win rights for Americans with disabilities eagerly awaited the changes the new law would bring. "I could taste the freedom," said McInnis. After being denied seats on trains and barred from restaurants because of her disability, the activist realized that with the passage of the act, "all those things became a reality, not just a dream."

People with disabilities looked forward to being able to pursue the same activities that other Americans enjoyed. "I envision a day," said Marilyn Golden, a policy analyst with the Disability Rights Education and Defense Fund, "when of course buildings will be accessible, of course public transit will be available, when the disabled can work, travel home, have vacations with their families."

She predicted that Americans would one day "look back and be astonished at what our world was once like, as we look back and are appalled at a time when we tolerated slavery and child labor."

Even with the law, advocates knew that people's stereotypes of those with disabilities would not disappear overnight. "You can't legislate attitudes," DREDF's Pat Wright told a reporter shortly before the passage of the ADA. "But the attitudinal barriers will drop the more disabled people are employed, the more they can be seen on the street and when we become not just a silent minority, but full participating members of society."

RELYING ON SCIENCE

Senate and House conferees spent the next month forging a law that both bodies could endorse. The most contentious difference was the Chapman amendment restricting people with AIDS and other "contagious diseases" from handling food. Not content to leave the outcome in the hands of the joint conference committee, Senator Jesse Helms pushed through a resolution supporting the amendment on June 6 in the Senate. Though nonbinding, the action put pressure on Senate negotiators to keep the amendment, which ADA sponsor Senator Harkin said would "codify ignorance." Harkin said the amendment struck "right to the heart and soul" of the ADA. People with disabilities, he said, "should not be judged nor discriminated against based on unfounded fear, prejudice, ignorance, or mythologies; people ought to be judged based upon the relevant medical evidence and the abilities they have."

Enraged disability rights activists immediately protested the Senate action. Most said they were willing to abandon the bill if it allowed discrimination against people with AIDS. Pat Wright expressed the views of the coalition when she said, "Fifty years ago, people wouldn't let their kids go to school with children who were mentally retarded, saying their children might catch it. Everyone who is disabled has to deal with this kind of prejudice."

Conference members spent days going through each segment of the Chapman amendment and working out joint positions. On June 25 conferees from both the Senate and the House voted to reject the amendment. It was a tough call for some, since they had to go against the majority of both the House and the Senate, who had voted in favor of the amendment. But retaining the measure threatened the survival of the ADA, and the majority of the conference members did not want the entire bill to fail. The following day, June 26, they completed their report and submitted the newly crafted bill to the House and the Senate.

In the meantime advocates on both sides of the controversy bombarded Congress with letters, telephone calls, and personal visits to persuade members to vote their way. Helms made it known that he would call for the Senate to include the Chapman amendment when it met to consider the final bill.

Republicans played a vital role in eliminating the amendment once and for all. On June 24 administration officials announced President Bush's opposition to the Chapman amendment. Conservative Utah senator Orrin Hatch became the key to resolving the situation. As the leading Republican at the Senate conference, Hatch had argued to keep the Chapman amendment. Disability rights activists Wright and Robert Silverstein convinced him that the ADA should not include a provision that discriminated against a group of people based on rumors and fear. If allowed to stand, they said, the amendment would kill the ADA.

Hatch crafted another amendment to take the place of the Chapman provision. His version gave the secretary of Health and Human Services the responsibility of issuing an annual list of communicable diseases that would pose a threat to the public if those with the illness handled food. The secretary had already issued a statement saying that food handlers with AIDS did not jeopardize the public. Under the measure, employers could reassign food handlers who had a disease on the list.

"We send a loud message that we are not just going to rely on blind fear as a basis for decision," Hatch declared when he introduced the amendment to the Senate on July 11. "Instead, we clarify that we are going to rely on the best available science." Later that day the Senate rejected Helms's measure and resoundingly approved the Hatch amendment. Helms cast the only vote against it.

OPENING DOORS TO ALL WITH DISABILITIES

That cleared the way for the final votes on the ADA. During debate in the House the next day, several conservative members argued for retaining the Chapman amendment. With the Hatch amendment as an alternative, however, the majority voted against the original measure, with a vote of 224 to 180. Many members urged support for the ADA even if they objected to some of its provisions. "We stand poised on the threshold of a bold new day for those Americans with disabilities," Representative Augustus Hawkins, Democrat from California, who chaired the House Committee on Education and Labor, told his colleagues. "Don't hold back the dawn of this equality over a minor provision of little weight. Let us pass this bill now, and tell all Americans we are glad to have you with us."

Representative Major Owens, Democrat from New York, said that many of his constituents referred to the legislation as "the hope bill." He, too, urged Congress to pass the ADA. In his concluding remarks, Representative Hoyer noted the importance of the ADA. "We are on the brink of enacting an independence bill for the disabled of America. They will henceforth, I think, look to this day and the day when the President of the United States signs this bill as the independence day for those who have been disabled but who have a willingness, a desire, and who are qualified and have an ability to productively participate in America, in the promise of America and in the pursuit of happiness."

Hoyer included in his remarks a tribute to Tony Coelho, the original sponsor of the bill, who had resigned from his House seat the year before. "This bill, in large measure, was the product of his devotion and of his faithfulness and of his commitment to making sure that the disabled of America were considered full participating citizens in our country," Hoyer said of Coelho.

Later that night, on July 12, 1990, the House voted 377 to 28 to accept the compromise bill. The following morning, a rainy day in Washington, D.C., the Senate began its final deliberations on the ADA. Excitement mounted as senator after senator rose to extol the virtues of the bill. Senator Hatch predicted that "every Senator in this Chamber will feel the floors shake as thunderous applause breaks out around America following our approval of the conference report on the Americans With Disabilities Act." Several speakers made reference to other monumental steps taken toward freedom around the globe in 1990: the collapse of the Soviet Union and the freeing of South African leader Nelson Mandela.

Senator Harkin recalled the testimony of a veteran disabled in the Vietnam War who told senators, "I did my job when I was called on by my country. Now it is your job and the job of everyone in Congress to make sure when I lost the use of my legs I didn't lose my ability to achieve my dreams." Harkin said that by passing the ADA, senators would meet the veteran's challenge. The senator then sent a special message to his brother Frank in sign language that "today was my proudest day in 16 years in Congress; that today Congress opens the doors to all Americans with disabilities; that today we say no to fear, that we say no to ignorance, and that we say no to prejudice."

Senator Hatch closed the debate with an emotional tribute

to his late brother-in-law, Raymond Hansen, who lost the use of his legs after a bout with polio as a college student. With his voice cracking and tears coursing down his cheeks, the long-term senator praised Hansen's courage as he faced his disability, earned a master's degree in electrical engineering, and, despite having to spend every night enclosed in an iron lung—a machine to assist his breathing—worked "right up to the day he died." Calling the passage of the ADA "a major achievement," Hatch said it showed the nation's determination to "go to the farthest lengths to make sure that everyone has equality and that everyone has a chance in this society."

At 9:34 a.m., the Senate formally endorsed the Americans with Disabilities Act, voting 91 to 6 to approve the bill. As Hatch had predicted, those in the packed galleries greeted the action with thunderous applause.

"WE HAVE DONE A LOT"

After the final vote, Kathryn McInnis called her mother in Saco, Maine, to tell her of the victory. "Honey, you're part of history; nothing is better than that," her mother told her. When McInnis began listing the law's flaws, Jean McInnis stilled her criticisms. Because of the law, she said, "some child is going to have the rights that you never had and that I fought so hard for you to have." McInnis followed her mother's suggestion to celebrate by visiting the monuments to Thomas Jefferson and Abraham Lincoln. At midnight she sat on the National Mall and thought, "We have done a lot."

Others shared that view. Justin Dart Jr. called the ADA "the world's first declaration of equality for people with disabilities" and said it proclaimed "to America and to the world that people with disabilities are fully human; that paternalistic, discriminatory, segregationist attitudes are no longer

From left front, Representative Steny Hoyer; Senator Orrin Hatch, wiping a tear of joy; Justin Dart Jr., wearing hat; and Yoshiko Dart, standing behind her husband, celebrate the passage of the ADA with others in 1990.

acceptable; and that henceforth people with disabilities must be accorded the same personal respect and the same social and economic opportunities as other people."

Senator Kennedy called the law "one of the most important accomplishments in the history of Congress."

On July 26, 1990, President George H. W. Bush officially signed the Americans with Disabilities Act. More than three thousand people—many of them in wheelchairs—witnessed the event, the largest signing ceremony in the country's history. The White House almost canceled the ceremony because officials feared the crowds and the weather would put too much strain on the many people with disabilities expected to attend. Even with the bill's passage, one of the most insidious barriers to people with disabilities—paternalistic attitudes that those with disabilities had to be taken care of—persisted. Evan J. Kemp Jr., adviser to the president and chair of the Equal Employment Opportunity Commission, who used a wheelchair himself, discounted officials' concerns. People with disabilities attending the ceremony "could be expected to take care of themselves," Kemp assured the worriers. They could deal with the heat, "just like other people," he said. If it rained, he added, they could "wear raincoats, use umbrellas and, if all else fails, come out of the rain just like anyone else."

The sun shone down on the huge gathering as those in the crowd—people with and without disabilities—cheered, hugged one another, and shed tears of joy. People who had been asked to leave restaurants, who had been barred from public schools and kept off buses now embraced this day of promise and equality. Justin Dart Jr., an official witness to the signing of the landmark legislation, sat in his wheelchair next to the president as Yoshiko Dart danced on the grass and exclaimed, "This is what's so great about America." The moment marked a turning point, a national recognition that Americans with disabilities would at last be guaranteed the civil rights enjoyed by other citizens.

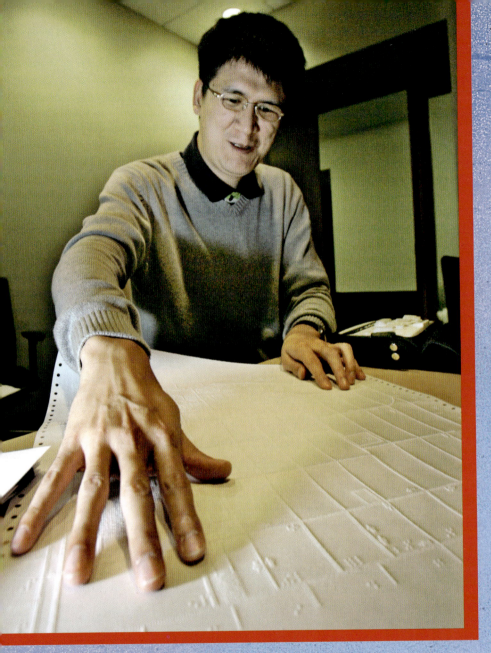

Sangyun Hahn, the first blind doctoral candidate in computer science at the University of Washington, uses his fingers in January 2005 to review a tactile campus map created by an undergraduate.

CHAPTER SIX

A New World

The passage of the Americans with Disabilities Act changed the lives of people with disabilities nationwide. Overnight they attained the same rights as other Americans to pursue happiness and a full life. Although discrimination was not eradicated, the act gave Americans with disabilities the tools to fight against it. "We changed thousands of lives," said Henry Viscardi Jr., a disability rights pioneer, in 1998. "I think it's a better world now than when [the campaign for rights] began. Far more disabled people are given the opportunity to be educated and to work."

When the law was passed in 1990, it affected 43 million Americans with disabilities—more than a sixth of the population, a number that would grow with each passing year. The legislation had an impact on an estimated 3.9 million businesses and 666,000 employers, according to the *New York Times.*

In the first decade of the twenty-first century, more than

50 million Americans have disabilities. As the baby boomer generation ages, that number is expected to increase rapidly. Almost every family has at least one member who is dealing with disabilities.

Things have definitely changed for the better, but there's a long way to go yet. A Harris poll conducted in 2003 revealed that only 32 percent of Americans with disabilities had jobs, while 81 percent of their nondisabled counterparts were employed. Slightly more than half—56 percent—of people with disabilities who said they could work had jobs. Of those who were employed, 36 percent had experienced discrimination, including being turned down for a job because of their disability.

Disability rights advocates note that workers with disabilities often are loyal, committed employees who appreciate the chance to have a job. Several national firms recruit workers with disabilities for that reason. While they still face difficulties in getting hired, once workers with disabilities are on the payroll, they are not laid off more often than other workers, according to Jim Weisman, attorney for the Eastern Paralyzed Veterans Association. "If you're competent, then your employer wants to keep you," he said. "Employers are more interested in competence than whether you're disabled."

TECHNOLOGICAL ADVANCES

The advances made in computer technology have greatly enhanced the ability of workers with disabilities to compete in the marketplace. Computers that talk have allowed blind users to make use of the technology for work and personal purposes. People who have lost the use of their hands can operate computers by other means, through voice or by using a mouth stick or a head stick. Those with debilitating conditions can work from home, using computers to connect them to the world. Deaf people can use special software that enables them to speak to others through the computer.

"The computer is allowing us to look at the disabled as people who can, rather than as people who cannot," said Alan Brightman, founder of Apple Computer's special education department. "Nondisabled individuals are able to see disabled peers in brand new ways, and disabled individuals see themselves in brand new ways." One software company official told of a boy with cerebral palsy, unable to speak or use a pen, who wrote a novel with the help of a computer.

People with disabilities still face a number of barriers when using computers, however. The cost of special hardware or software may be too expensive for private individuals and the self-employed. Deaf computer users complain that many of the videos available on the Internet have no captions. Blind people face additional challenges in dealing with websites, a vast majority of which are not compatible with the software that reads material aloud. In February 2006 blind consumers filed a class-action suit against Target because their access to the store's website was blocked. By not programming its website to be compatible with screen-reader technology, the suit charged, Target was discriminating against blind consumers and violating the ADA. Target reached an agreement with the plaintiffs in August 2008 that required the store to make all its websites accessible to blind users by February 2009. Google, the giant Internet search engine, has made access a priority and has even developed a service that gives a slight edge to sites that are accessible. Engineers are working on a variety of products that will help make it easier for people with disabilities to gain access to the Internet.

SEEING THE WORLD

Leisure businesses have discovered a profitable market in catering to people with disabilities. Once confined to special living centers or their own homes, many people with disabilities are venturing forth to see the world. Specialty travel companies offer tours to accommodate people with a range of disabilities, even providing medical equipment for those requiring kidney dialysis or oxygen tanks. Cruise lines are increasingly building or refitting ships to accommodate wheelchairs. A study conducted in 2003 reported that 11 million Americans with disabilities went on trips at least yearly and paid nearly $13.5 billion in travel costs.

Plenty of hurdles remain, however. Bathroom doors in some hotels are not wide enough for wheelchairs to pass through. Not all airplanes have bathrooms that are accessible, and narrow aisles cannot accommodate standard-sized wheelchairs. Subways, taxis, and rental cars present their own barriers to people with disabilities. "The worst place on earth for the disabled is a place called New York City," said Tony Schrader, a quadriplegic who has traveled the world.

Despite victories in the courts, many people with disabilities cannot rely on public buses in their area. Not all buses are equipped with wheelchair lifts, and often the lifts do not work or drivers refuse to operate them. Rus Cooper-Dowda, a minister in St. Petersburg, Florida, related the experience of one frustrated rider who relied on the bus to get to work each day. More than ten years after ADA's passage, a driver could not find the correct switch to activate the wheelchair lift. On another day a driver refused to move the bus to more level ground so that the lift would work. On yet another day, a driver laughed when the lift did not work, refused to report the malfunction to company headquarters, and commented to the waiting rider, "You didn't really want to go to work anyway, did you?" She did want to go to work, but the bus drove off without her.

COURTS POSE THREAT TO ADA

In recent years the Supreme Court has upheld protections against discrimination for prisoners with disabilities, ordered states to pay for private-school tuition for students with disabilities whose needs were not being met by public schools, and expanded ADA coverage to people with mental disabilities and those with AIDS and HIV.

Other rulings, however, have narrowed the definition of who qualifies as disabled under the ADA and the steps that must be taken to accommodate workers with disabilities. Justices ruled in three 1999 cases that people who could perform their job if they took their medication or took other measures, such as wearing a prosthetic leg or donning glasses, would not be protected under the ADA. A 5-to-4 decision in a 2001 case, *Board of Trustees of the University of Alabama* v. *Garrett*, barred state workers from collecting damages in ADA lawsuits. In a 2002 case the Court redefined a person with disabilities as one whose limitations were "central to daily life." Conditions that affected a person's ability to perform a job but not his or her fulfillment of "major life activities" did not fall under the protection of the ADA, according to the ruling in *Toyota Motor Manufacturing, Kentucky, Inc.* v. *Williams*. Employers considered the decision to be a major victory. Another decision that year gave employers the right to reject job applicants with disabilities whose health or safety might be jeopardized by the work.

During the 2004 presidential campaign, former congressman Tony Coelho, who had first introduced the ADA in the

House, warned that the law was "under savage attack in the courts." In addition, he said, the ADA's provisions protecting the rights of workers with disabilities were "being whittled away and we must restore them."

The court cases spurred the National Council on Disability to action. The council held hearings on recent Supreme Court cases and issued a report on how the Court's rulings had distorted the intent of Congress when it enacted the ADA. The report, titled *Righting the ADA*, also proposed ways to address the problem. In particular it urged rewording the definition of "disability" so that it included "any physical or mental impairment."

SAVING THE ADA

The council's report helped ignite another campaign, this time to save the ADA. Many of the same players took part in the new effort, including the Consortium for Citizens with Disabilities and the two lead politicians in the past battle, Senator Tom Harkin and Representative Steny Hoyer. They were joined by a key Republican, Representative Jim Sensenbrenner, who agreed to sponsor a bill to preserve the ADA. On September 29, 2006, Representatives Sensenbrenner, Hoyer, and John Conyers Jr. (Democrat of Michigan) cosponsored the ADA Restoration Act.

As before, the coalition sought input for the new law and support for it from members of the disability rights community across the nation. The bill was resubmitted to the 110th Congress on July 26, 2007, seventeen years after Congress passed the first ADA. As the bill wound its way through the various committees, it picked up support. By January 2008, it had attracted 247 cosponsors in the House. By the time the bill became law, that number had grown to 255. These supporters were met with strong opposition from business lobbyists and President George W. Bush, son of the president who signed and supported the original bill.

Representatives from the disability rights community and business groups met in February to negotiate the terms of the bill. Thirteen weeks later the negotiation team delivered a modified bill that both sides could live with. The compromise measure, known as the ADA Amendments Act of 2008, included the following changes:

- Those taking medication or other steps to treat a disability would not be excluded from protections.
- The ADA would cover people who were "substantially limited in one major life activity," even if they were able to perform many other tasks.
- A person would be covered even for disabilities in remission or recurring intermittently.
- People would be covered by the law if they were treated unfairly because of a perceived disability.
- Employers would not be required to make accommodations for people merely regarded as disabled.

The revised bill reinstated the definition of disability present in the original ADA: that a person with an impairment that "substantially limited" a "major life activity" was considered disabled. It also clarified other terms in the bill.

In September 2008, with support from business and disability groups, the ADA Amendments Act of 2008 passed by unanimous consent in the Senate and by voice vote in the House. On September 25, President George W. Bush signed the bill into law as his father looked on. The act overturned several Supreme Court decisions that had weakened the ADA and threatened the rights of people with disabilities. Senator Harkin, who ushered the original bill and the new act through the legislative process, said the new bill would "restore the original promise and protections of the ADA."

FILING A DISCRIMINATION COMPLAINT

The Equal Employment Opportunity Commission (EEOC) handled more than 95,000 complaints in 2008, and more than 19,000 involved disability discrimination claims. Since the passage of the ADA, the number of work discrimination cases settled in favor of workers with disabilities has steadily risen. Between 1996 and 2001, for example, the number of workers with disabilities who won employment discrimination complaints rose by 103 percent. In cases involving all types of illegal discrimination, plaintiffs represented by an attorney won 38.3 percent of verdicts issued after a trial and lost only 13.2 percent of cases settled out of court. When the EEOC took a case to court on behalf of an employee, the commission won more than half of the time. The commission lost only 5.9 percent of cases settled out of court.

A CONSTANT STRUGGLE

Still, Americans with disabilities must often take action to ensure that their rights are protected. From October 1, 2007, to September 30, 2008, the EEOC handled 19,453 discrimination cases filed by people with disabilities. Of those, the commission resolved 16,705 charges and recovered $57.2 million in lost wages and other revenue for those who had been discriminated against because of their disabilities. That figure does not include money awarded in court cases pursued by plaintiffs. Local and state commissions also handle numerous complaints about discrimination. The commissions at all levels encourage workers and employers to resolve disputes through mediation. Filing a complaint and using the EEOC's mediation services are free. Cases take months, sometimes years, to resolve.

The EEOC investigates charges and attempts to resolve cases through mediation or other method before issuing a ruling. If the EEOC rules that discrimination has occurred, workers may take their case to federal court with their own lawyer. Some lawyers will argue the case on a contingency basis, collecting their fee from the proceeds of the awards in successful suits. Organizations like the Disability Rights Education and Defense Fund sometimes help with legal fees in big cases. In a few cases the EEOC itself will take a case to court when an issue affects many employees or the discrimination is extremely severe. Of the thousands of complaints filed, the commission sues in only about 350 cases a year. Most cases are settled through mediation.

"Freedom is a constant struggle," observed Kathryn McInnis, who now uses her married name of McInnis-Misenor. Like many others, she continues to fight discrimination wherever she encounters it. After the birth of her daughter, Sara, in 1999, she and her husband sued the medical center in an effort to force it to make the birthing rooms accessible to mothers in wheelchairs. After an initial defeat in federal court, McInnis won the right to pursue the case in Maine Superior Court and eventually accepted a negotiated settlement that satisfied both sides. Today all of the hospital's labor and delivery and post-delivery rooms are accessible, a spokesperson for the medical center said. McInnis-Misenor has also spent many hours educating people about disability rights and what it means to be a person with disabilities.

Filing a Claim

A worker who believes he or she has been discriminated against because of a disability should first discuss the matter with the company's human resources department. If that does not resolve the situation, the worker should file a complaint with the Equal Employment Opportunity Commission (EEOC) within 180 to 300 days of the incident, depending on the circumstances. The worker may also want to consult a lawyer, although no lawyer is required to file a complaint.

Most complaints filed with the EEOC take several months to resolve and are settled out of court. Workers must prove that wrongful actions have been taken against them, such as being fired or not hired because of a disability. Experts advise workers to keep a diary or record of actions, behavior, and words to use in their case.

Once the complaint, or charge, has been filed, the EEOC arranges mediation between the worker and the employer. If one or both of the parties refuse to go to mediation or to accept the results, the EEOC will review the case and rule on whether there is probable cause for a lawsuit. In cases where probable cause is found, employers often agree to settle a dispute to avoid legal action. If that does not take place, the EEOC issues the complainant a notice that allows him or her to take the case to federal court. In cases that affect many people or deal with the worst instances of discrimination, the EEOC may take the violator to court.

When state or federal agencies violate the accessibility regulations of the Americans with Disabilities Act, citizens may take the case to court without obtaining a "right to sue" notice. Alternatively, they may file a complaint with the Department of Justice, which may take the matter to mediation. Complaints may also be filed with the Justice Department regarding violations involving public transportation and public accommodations, such as restaurants and businesses. In some situations, the Justice Department may sue the violator. The Civil Rights Division of the Justice Department can refer people to the relevant agency to file complaints against violations of other provisions of the ADA.

"Laws can do a lot," she said, "but change really has to come from within." While her daughter's school was handicapped-accessible during school hours, the wheelchair entrance was locked when McInnis-Misenor came for a parent conference. School officials had to be reminded that the building needed to be accessible to parents as well as students. She has encountered several instances of prejudice or ignorance. A stranger at the grocery store exclaimed that McInnis's fiancé must be a saint for asking her to marry him. One man accused her of breastfeeding another woman's child when he saw her caring for her infant.

Such hurtful comments can discourage the most resolute of people. A constant barrage of such talk has led some people with disabilities to question their own capabilities. McInnis-Misenor, who has served as a mentor to many with disabilities, encourages them to meet challenges head-on and use the legal tools they have been given to make things better. "If you talk the talk, then roll the walk," she said with a smile. "The best revenge is living a truly independent, empowered life."

During the long battle for equal rights and the ensuing victory attained with the passage of the ADA, many Americans' concepts of people with disabilities have changed. While not everyone has learned the lesson that people with disabilities can lead full lives, many have embraced that fact. McInnis-Misenor recalled the day almost three decades ago when she had to be carried up two flights of stairs to take her seat on the city council. Today she can easily wheel herself into city hall and take an elevator to the council chambers. With many barriers down, Americans now encounter more people with disabilities and understand that they are just like everyone else. "That fact," said McInnis-Misenor, "is now embedded in the hearts and minds of the next generation."

From Bill to Law

For a proposal to become a federal law, it must go through many steps:

In Congress:

1. A bill is proposed by a citizen, a legislator, the president, or another interested party. Most bills originate in the House and then are considered in the Senate.

2. A representative submits the bill to the House (the first reading). A senator submits it to the Senate. The person (or people) who introduces the bill is its main sponsor. Other lawmakers can become sponsors to show support for the bill. Each bill is read three times before the House or the Senate.

3. The bill is assigned a number and referred to the committee(s) and subcommittee(s) dealing with the topic. Each committee adopts its own rules, following guidelines of the House and the Senate. The committee chair controls scheduling for the bill.

4. The committees hold hearings if the bill is controversial or complex. Experts and members of the public may testify. Congress may compel witnesses to testify if they do not do so voluntarily.

5. The committee reviews the bill, discusses it, adds amendments, and makes other changes it deems necessary during markup sessions.

6. The committee votes on whether to support the bill, oppose it, or take no action on it and issues a report on its findings and recommendations.

7. A bill that receives a favorable committee report goes to the Rules Committee to be scheduled for consideration by the full House or Senate.

8. If the committee delays a bill or if the Rules Committee fails to schedule it, House members can sign a discharge motion and call for a vote on the matter. If a majority votes to release the bill from committee, it is scheduled on the calendar as any other bill would be. Senators may vote to discharge the bill from a committee as well. More commonly, though, a senator will add the bill as an amendment to an unrelated bill in order to get it past the committee blocking it. Or a senator can request that a bill be put directly on the Senate calendar, where it will be scheduled for debate. House and Senate members can also vote to suspend the rules and vote directly on a bill. Bills passed in this way must receive support from two thirds of those voting.

9. Members of both houses debate the bill. In the House, a chairperson moderates the discussion and each speaker's time is limited. Senators can speak on the issue for as long as they wish. Senators who want to block the bill may debate for hours in a tactic known as a filibuster. A three-fifths vote of the Senate is required to stop the filibuster (cloture), and talk on the bill is then limited to one hour per senator.

10. Following the debate, the bill is read section by section (the second reading). Members may propose amendments, which are voted on before the final bill comes up for a vote.

11. The full House and Senate then debate the entire bill and those amendments approved previously. Debate continues until a majority of members vote to "move the previous question" or approve a special resolution forcing a vote.

12. A full quorum—at least 218 members in the House, 51 in the Senate—must be present for a vote to be held. A member may request a formal count of members to ensure a quorum is on hand. Absent members are sought when there is no quorum.

13. Before final passage, opponents are given a last chance to propose amendments that alter the bill; the members vote on them.

14. A bill needs approval from a majority of those voting to pass. Members who do not want to take a stand on the issue may choose to abstain (not vote at all) or merely vote present.

15. If the House passes the bill, it goes on to the Senate. By that time, bills often have more than one hundred amendments attached to them. Occasionally, a Senate bill will go to the House.

16. If the bill passes in the same form in both the House and the Senate, it is sent to the clerk to be recorded.

17. If the Senate and the House version differ, the Senate sends the bill to the House with the request that members approve the changes.

18. If the two houses disagree on the changes, the bill may go to conference, where members appointed by the House and the Senate work out a compromise if possible.

19. The House and the Senate vote on the revised bill agreed to in conference. Further amendments may be added and the process repeated if the Senate and the House version of the bill differ.

20. The bill goes to the president for a signature.

To the President:

1. If the president signs the bill, it becomes law.

2. If the president vetoes the bill, it goes back to Congress, which can override his veto with a two-thirds vote in both houses.

3. If the president takes no action, the bill automatically becomes law after ten days if Congress is still in session.

4. If Congress adjourns and the president has taken no action on the bill within ten days, it does not become law. This is known as a pocket veto.

The time from introduction of the bill to the signing can range from several months to the entire two-year session. If a bill does not win approval during the session, it can be reintroduced in the next Congress, where it will have to go through the whole process again.

Notes

Introduction

p. 8, "Our society . . . is still infected . . .": Justin Dart, "ADA: Landmark Declaration of Equality," *Worklife*, September 22, 1990, www.accessmylibrary.com/coms2/summary_0286-9221083_ITM.

p. 8, "'As disabled,' Dart observed, 'we had to . . .'": Mary Ann Farrell, "Justin Dart Widely Acclaimed as Leading Advocate for Disabled Rights Movement," Knight-Ridder/Tribune News Service, June 10, 1994.

p. 9, "a strong and inspiring coalition . . .": George H. W. Bush, "Remarks of President George Bush at the Signing of the Americans with Disabilities Act," July 26, 1990, U.S. EEOC, www.eeoc.gov/abouteeoc/35th/videos/ada_signing_text.html.

p. 9, "the world's first comprehensive declaration . . .": News Services, "Springs Women See 'Independence Day'/ Bush Signs Law to Aid Handicapped," *Colorado Springs Gazette-Telegraph*, July 27, 1990, A1.

p. 9, "Let the shameful wall of exclusion . . .": "Bush Signs Bill to Outlaw Bias Against Disabled," *Austin American Statesman*, July 27, 1990, A1.

pp. 10–11, "ADA of 1990," U.S. Equal Employment Opportunity Commission (EEOC), www.eeoc.gov/abouteeoc/35th/thelaw/ada.html.

p. 12, "is not a law about disabilities . . .": Andrew Gomes, quoted in Silvia Yee and Marilyn Golden, "Achieving Accessibility: How the Americans with Disabilities Act Is Changing the Face and Mind of a Nation," Disability Rights Education & Defense Fund, www.dredf.org/international/paper_y-g.html#_ftn114.

Chapter One

p. 13, "For all [the bill's] flaws, . . .": Kathryn McInnis-Misenor, interview with the author, October 1, 2008.

p. 16, "We didn't ask her to run, . . .": Gary L. Robbins, "Brand-new Saco Councilor at Center of City Hall Uproar," *Journal Tribune*, November 6, 1980, 10.

p. 16, "If I were handicapped, I . . .": Gary L. Robbins, "Councilor Wins Fight to Change Meeting Places," *Journal Tribune*, November 25, 1980, 1.

pp. 16–17, "I am aware every day of physical . . .": Kathy McInnis, Letter to the Editor, *Journal Tribune*, November 11, 1980, 4.

p. 17, "Rehabilitation Act of 1973": U.S. Congress, *Rehabilitation Act of 1973, Public Law 93-112*, 93rd Congress, H. R. 8070, September 26, 1973.

pp. 17–18, "Letter writers assailed the council's position . . .": Letters to the Editor, *Journal Tribune*, November 8, 9, 10, 13, 1980, 4.

p. 18, "deplorable lack of compassion and . . .": Editorial, "McInnis: Her Legal Rights of Access," *Journal Tribune*, November 13, 1980, 4.

p. 18, "that until very recently called . . .": Editorial, "McInnis: Her Legal Rights of Access," November 13, 1980.

pp. 18, 20, "The integration of handicapped and . . .": Robbins, "Councilor Wins Fight to Change Meeting Places," November 25, 1980.

p. 20, "All of us who were there . . .": McInnis-Misenor, interview with the author.

Chapter Two

p. 21, "As a result of those beliefs . . .": W. Roy Grizzard, "Impact of Disability History, Identity and Community—Yesterday, Today and Tomorrow," 2004 National Youth Leadership Conference speech, U.S. Department of Labor Office of Disability Employment Policy, July 26, 2004. www.dol.gov/odep/media/speeches/youth.htm.

p. 22, "the most disgraceful memorials of . . .": John E. B. Myers, *Child Protection in America: Past, Present, and Future*, New York: Oxford University Press, 2006, 13.

p. 22, "Society viewed people disabled . . .": U.S. Department of Veterans Affairs, "History of the Department of Veterans Affairs—Part 1," February 11, 2008, www1.va.gov/opa/feature/history/history1.asp.

p. 22, "should be kept diffused among sound . . .": James C. Harris, *Intellectual Disability: Understanding its Development, Causes, Classification, Evaluation, and Treatment*, New York: Oxford University Press, 2006, 19.

p. 23, "cheerful and even gay . . .": Elliott and Hall, *Laura Bridgman*, 235–236.

p. 23, "One of Laura's first accomplishments . . .": Elliott and Hall, *Laura Bridgman*, 235–236.

pp. 23–24, "Teachers at the school . . .": Elliott and Hall, *Laura Bridgman*, 235–236.

p. 25, "Anne Sullivan, a graduate of the . . .": Kimberly French, "Samuel Gridley Howe: Champion of the Blind," *UU World*, Unitarian Universalist Association, January/February 2005.

p. 26, "Howe believed that once these students . . .": French, "Samuel Gridley Howe." January/February 2005.

p. 26, "Much can be done for them . . .": Maud Howe Elliott and Florence Howe Hall, *Laura Bridgman: Dr. Howe's Famous Pupil and What He Taught Her*, Boston: Little, Brown, and Company, 1903, 13–14.

pp. 27–28, "Those with disabilities continued . . .": U.S. Holocaust Memorial Museum Panel Presentation, "The Nazi Persecution of Deaf People," Center for Advanced Holocaust Studies, August 2001, www.ushmm.org/museum/exhibit/focus/disabilities_02.

pp. 28–29, "In the 1960s sociologist Erving Goffman . . .": Erving Goffman, *Stigma: Notes on the Management of Spoiled Identity*, New York: Simon & Schuster, 1963, 3.

p. 29, "Nondisabled people often treated . . .": Goffman, *Stigma*, 3.

p. 29, "They would never look me in the face . . .": Kathryn McInnis-Misenor, interview with the author, October 1, 2008.

p. 29, "When McInnis was pregnant with her daughter . . .": McInnis-Misenor, interview with the author.

p. 29, "They, too, tended to see . . .": McInnis-Misenor, interview with the author.

p. 31, "strength and inspiration . . .": Meghan Mutchler, "Roosevelt's Disability an Issue at Memorial," *New York Times*, April 10, 1995.

p. 31, "This is a monument to freedom . . .": William Clinton, "Remarks on the Unveiling of a Statue at the Franklin D. Roosevelt Memorial," Washington, D.C., January 10, 2001, www.presidency.ucsb.edu/ws/index.php?pid=65051.

p. 32, "During World War II, Congress passed . . .": U.S. Department of Veterans Affairs, "History of the Department of Veterans Affairs—Part 4," www1.va.gov/opa/feature/history/history4.asp.

p. 32, "I had to give up . . .": Kenneth Sawtelle, interview with author, September 1996.

pp. 32–33, "Paralyzed and in a wheelchair . . .": Bryan Marquard, "Charlie Sabatier; Helped Win Access, Respect for Disabled," *Boston Globe*, June 12, 2009, www.boston.com/bostonglobe/obituaries/articles/2009/06/12/charlie_sabatier_helped_win_access_respect_for_disabled.

Chapter Three

p. 37, "Republican president . . . own social programs": Paul K. Longmore, *Why I Burned My Book and Other Essays on Disability*, Philadelphia: Temple University Press, 2003, 103–104.

p. 37, "aware of the plight . . .": "Disabled Tie Up Traffic Here to Protest Nixon Aid-Bill Vote," *New York Times*, November 3, 1972, 43.

p. 37, "'After all,' he told the *New York Times*, 'there can't be . . .'": Marjorie Hunter, "Congress Votes Bill Facing Veto; Aid to Handicapped Children Chosen for Initial Test of Strength," *New York Times*, March 16, 1973, 19.

p. 37, "a hollow victory . . .": "A Hollow Victory," *New York Times*, April 11, 1977, 12.

p. 38, "a physical or mental disability which . . .": U.S. Congress, *Rehabilitation Act of 1973, Public Law 93-112*, 93rd Congress, H. R. 8070, September 26, 1973.

p. 38, "[A]ny person who (i) has a . . .": *School Board of Nassau County, Florida, et al.* v. *Arline*, 480 U.S. 273, 1987; Rehabilitation Act of 1973, Sections 501 and 505, "Definitions," as amended, 1974.

p. 39, "From 1975 to 1977 workers with . . .": Jerry Flint, "Civil Rights: Handicapped No Longer Act Like It," *New York Times*, October 2, 1977, E8.

p. 40, "The Department's failure . . .": Nancy Hicks, "Handicapped Use Protests to Push H.E.W. to Implement '73 Bias Law," *New York Times*, April 29, 1977, NJ1.

p. 41, "We believe we have won . . .": Nancy Hicks, "Califano Signs Regulations to Ban Discriminations Against Disabled," *New York Times*, April 29, 1977, NJ1.

p. 41, "'reasonable accommodations' to the workplace . . .": Hicks, "Califano Signs Regulations," April 29, 1977.

p. 41, "the recognition of the Congress . . .": Hicks, "Califano Signs Regulations," April 29, 1977.

p. 42, "free appropriate public education . . .": U.S. Office of Special Programs, "History: Twenty-Five Years of Progress in Educating Children with Disabilities Through IDEA," Washington, D.C.: U.S. Department of Education, 2000, www.ed.gov/policy/speced/leg/idea/history.pdf.

p. 43, "During the first four months of 1978 . . .": Steven V. Roberts, "The Handicapped Are Emerging as a Vocal Political Action Group," *New York Times*, June 19, 1978, A16.

p. 44, "because their disability might cause . . .": Janet Elder, "Disabled View Their Gains," *New York Times*, May 21, 1986.

p. 44, "content to be supported by the government . . .": Elder, "Disabled View Their Gains," May 21, 1986.

p. 44, "philosophy that . . . 'new federalism' . . .": Austin Hoyt, "Ronald Reagan, 40th President," *American Experience*, Public Broadcasting Service, 1998, www.pbs.org/wgbh/amex/presidents/40_reagan/reagan_domestic.html.

p. 46, "To spend millions for elevators to satisfy . . .": "Koch Blocks Accord on Subway Access for Disabled People," *New York Times*, June 22, 1984, 1.

Chapter Four

p. 48, "'legitimate physical requirements' . . .": *Southeastern Community College* v. *Davis*, 442 U.S. 397, 1979.

p. 48, "I am deeply afraid that many colleges . . .": Gene I. Maeroff, "Quandary for the Colleges: Law Barring Discrimination Against Handicapped Could Force Expensive Alterations on Campus," *New York Times*, June 16, 1979, 19.

p. 48, "the line between a lawful refusal to extend . . .": Linda Greenhouse, "Deaf Student Loses High Court Appeal," *New York Times*, June 12, 1979, 1.

pp. 48–49, "We have found . . . spending the money,": Maeroff, "Quandary for the Colleges," June 16, 1979.

p. 49, "thoughtlessness and indifference": *Alexander* v. *Choate*, 469 U.S. 287, 1985.

p. 50, "drastic limitation on the handicapped . . .": *Consolidated Rail Corporation* v. *Darrone*, 465 U.S. 627, 1984.

pp. 50–51, "President Ronald Reagan used the *Grove City College* . . .": Martin Tolchin, "Civil Rights Plan Shelved as Senate Moves on Spending," *New York Times*, October 3, 1984, 1.

p. 51, "myths and fears about disability and disease . . .": *School Board of Nassau County, Florida, et al.* v. *Arline*, 480 U.S. 273, 1987.

p. 52, "200 Protesters, One Jail Cell": Mary Johnson and Barrett Shaw, *To Ride the Public's Buses: The Fight That Built a Movement*, Disability Rag Reader, Louisville, KY: Advocado Press, 2001, 151; and Leonard Sawisch, e-mail message to author, October 15, 2008.

p. 53, "Our rights, our dignity, our quality . . .": Associated Press, "Handicapped in Protest of 'Federalism' Policy," *New York Times*, May 1, 1982, 14; Kathryn McInnis-Misenor, interview with the author, October 1, 2008.

p. 54, "commitment to equal opportunity for disabled . . .": Jonathan M. Young, "Equality of Opportunity: The Making of the Americans with Disabilities Act," National Council on Disability, July 26, 1997, www.ncd.gov/newsroom/publications/1997/equality.htm.

p. 54, "developing the individual dignity and potential . . .": Associated Press, "Convention in Dallas: The Republicans; Excerpts from Platform Adopted by Republican Convention," *New York Times*, August 22, 1984, 19A.

p. 56, "Before, people had been pitted against each . . .": McInnis-Misenor, interview with the author.

p. 56, "More than five hundred people . . .": McInnis-Misenor, interview with the author.

p. 56, "equal access to places of public accommodation . . .": Associated Press, "New England News in Brief; Bus-Access Order Won by Handicapped," *Boston Globe*, August 15, 1984, 1.

p. 57, "Because public accommodations accessibility . . .": Associated Press, "New England News in Brief," August 15, 1984, 1.

p. 58, "My life no longer required two weeks or 72 . . .": McInnis-Misenor, interview with the author.

p. 58, "impacts state human rights acts nationwide . . .": Johnson and Shaw, *To Ride the Public's Buses*, 117.

pp. 58, 60, "modest, affirmative steps to accommodate handicapped persons . . .": Johnson and Shaw, *To Ride the Public's Buses*, 67.

p. 59, "Making a Difference": McInnis-Misenor, interview with the author.

p. 61, "Congress wanted to provide . . .": Associated Press, "Appeals Court Orders That Buses Be Fitted for Handicapped," *New York Times*, February 14, 1989.

p. 61, "SEPARATE IS NEVER EQUAL . . .": Johnson and Shaw, *To Ride the Public's Buses*, 153–155.

p. 62, "Only a mixed-system . . .": *Americans Disabled for Accessible Public Transportation* v. *Burnley*, 881 F.2d 1184, 58 USLW 2090, July 24, 1989, http://bulk.resource.org/courts.gov/c/F2/881/881.F2d.1184.88-1177.88-1139.88-1178.html.

p. 63, "the most effective advocate I have ever . . .": U.S. Congress, *Congressional Record*, 101st Cong., 2nd sess., July 13, 1990, S9698.

p. 64, "temporarily able-bodied": Susan F. Rasky, "How the Disabled Sold Congress on a New Bill of Rights," *New York Times*, September 17, 1989, Week in Review.

p. 64, "If we had not won on the Voting Rights . . .": Young, "Equality of Opportunity."

p. 65, "One of the first facilities . . .": Nancy Hicks, "Berkeley Turns Into Mecca for Handicapped Persons," *New York Times*, September 8, 1976, 16.

pp. 65–66, "An incredible amount of paternalism . . .": Steven V. Roberts, "The Handicapped Are Emerging As a Vocal Political Action Group," *New York Times*, June 19, 1978, A16.

p. 66, "Opponents tacked on . . .": Martin Tolchin, "Civil Rights Plan Shelved as Senate Moves on Spending," *New York Times*, October 3, 1984, 1.

p. 66, "'Shame on the Senate,' he said. 'We are being asked . . .'": Tolchin, "Civil Rights Plan Shelved as Senate Moves on Spending," October 3, 1984.

p. 67, "People who voluntarily take Federal funds . . .": Irvin Molotsky, "House and Senate Vote to Override Reagan on Rights," *New York Times*, March 23, 1988, 1.

p. 68, "Until now, the Federal Fair Housing . . .": Thomas J. Leuck, "The New Teeth in the Fair Housing Law," *New York Times*, March 12, 1989.

p. 68, "working relationships with members . . .": Young, "Equality of Opportunity."

Chapter Five

p. 70, "Fearing that Reagan would disband...": Jonathan M. Young, "Equality of Opportunity: The Making of the Americans with Disabilities Act," National Council on Disability, July 26, 1997, www.ncd.gov/newsroom/publications/1997/equality.htm.

p. 71, "requiring equal opportunity for individuals . . .": National Council on Disability, "Toward Independence: An Assessment of Federal Laws and Programs Affecting Persons with Disabilities—With Legislative Recommendations," February 1986, www.ncd.gov/newsroom/publications/1986/toward.htm#2.

p. 71, "If the goals of independence and access to . . .": National Council on Disability, "Toward Independence," February 1986,

pp. 72–73, "Justin Dart Jr., ADA's Godfather": Fred Fay and Fred Pelka, "Justin Dart—An Obituary," Disability Social History Project, June 22, 2002, www.disabilityhistory.org/people_dart.html; "Justin Dart, Jr. Legend in Disabilities Advocacy," *The Exceptional Parent*, August 1, 2002; and Mary Ann Farrell, "Justin Dart Widely Acclaimed as Leading Advocate for Disabled Rights Movement," Knight-Ridder/Tribune News Service, June 10, 1994.

p. 73, "I don't know that I've ever . . .": William Clinton, "President's Remarks on Justin Dart Jr.," Independent Living Research Utilization, January 15, 1998, www.ilru.org/html/about/Dart/remarks.html.

p. 73, "As he left the stage, Dart took the . . .": Karen G. Stone, "Justin Dart, Jr.—A Peek of Insight," Independent Living Institute, February 2001, www.independentliving.org/column/stone200102.html.

pp. 74–76, "The protest and victory at Gallaudet...": Young, "Equality of Opportunity," July 26, 1997.

p. 76, "If it had been one person against...": Young, "Equality of Opportunity," July 26, 1997.

p. 76, "I don't think we left them...": Kathryn McInnis-Misenor, interview with the author, October 1, 2008.

pp. 76–77, "It is high time that we as a...": U.S. Congress, *Congressional Record*, 100th Cong., 1st sess., April 28, 1988, S9379.

p. 77, "substantial and pervasive...": U.S. Congress, *Congressional Record*, April 28, 1988.

pp. 77–78, "Heumann, who had organized...": Senator Tom Harkin, U.S. Congress, Senate, *Congressional Record*, 103rd Cong., 1st sess., June 23, 1993, 43.

p. 78, "Another woman, Belinda Mason,...": Young, "Equality of Opportunity," July 26, 1997.

p. 78, "Others told of being turned away at...": Senator Tom Harkin, *Congressional Record*, June 23, 1993.

p. 78, "Bush had developed a respect...": Young, "Equality of Opportunity," July 26, 1997.

p. 79, "I didn't get elected to get...": Young, "Equality of Opportunity," July 26, 1997.

p. 79, "Senate staff members headed by Robert Silverstein . . .": Young, "Equality of Opportunity," July 26, 1997; and Kathryn McInnis-Misenor, interview with the author, October 1, 2008.

p. 81, "'undue hardship,' defined as 'unduly costly,'...": U.S. EEOC, *Americans with Disabilities Act of 1990*.

p. 82, "a physical or mental impairment that substantially . . .": *Americans with Disabilities Act of 1990*, U.S. EEOC.

p. 82, "the most critical legislation affecting persons with . . .": U.S. Congress, *Congressional Record*, 101st Cong., 1st sess., May 9, 1989, S4985–7.

p. 83, "This historic piece of legislation . . .": U.S. Congress, *Congressional Record*, May 9, 1989.

p. 84, "We can be productive if you . . .": Young, "Equality of Opportunity," July 26, 1997.

p. 85, "Harkin addressed the concerns...": U.S. Congress, *Congressional Record*, 101st Cong., 1st sess., May 9, 1989, S4985–7.

p. 85, "would free hundreds of thousands of . . .": James S. Brady, "Save Money: Help the Disabled," *New York Times*, August 29, 1989, op-ed page.

p. 86, "We're going to do whatever we . . .": Jason DeParle, "Realizing the Rights of the Disabled," *New York Times*, December 17, 1989, 1A.

p. 86, "The chairman of Greyhound . . .": DeParle, "Realizing the Rights of the Disabled," December 17, 1989.

pp. 86–87, "We're the faces of this movement . . .": Kathryn McInnis-Misenor, interview with the author.

p. 87, "There were a million little heroes around . . .": McInnis-Misenor, interview with the author.

p. 87, "full support for comprehensive . . .": Ronald J. Ostrow, "Rights for the Disabled: White House Backs Bill to Prohibit Discrimination," *Austin American Statesman*, June 23, 1989, 4A.

p. 88, "It makes no sense for a law . . .": Susan F. Rasky, "How the Disabled Sold Congress on a New Bill of Rights," *New York Times*, September 17, 1989, Week in Review.

p. 88, "We would never [have] gotten it . . .": Elizabeth Koblert, "As Candidate, Dole Casts Off His Feats as a Skilled Senator," *New York Times*, August 9, 1996, 1.

p. 89, "It was worth the trade-off . . .": Rasky, "How the Disabled Sold Congress on a New Bill of Rights," September 17, 1989.

pp. 89–90, "A U.S. Chamber of Commerce lawyer . . .": David C. Beeder, "Disabilities Act Near Hearings; Some Opposed," *Omaha–World Herald*, September 6, 1989, 10.

p. 90, "a wave of lawsuits . . .": Susan F. Rasky, "Bill Barring Bias Against Disabled Holds Wide Impact," *New York Times*, August 14, 1989.

p. 90, "the lawyers' employment act . . .": Editorial, "The Lawyers' Employment Act," *Wall Street Journal*, September 11, 1989, 1.

p. 90, "pedophiles, transsexuals, voyeurs and kleptomaniacs . . .": Editorial, "The Lawyers' Employment Act," September 11, 1989.

p. 91, "If it's too burdensome for the . . .": Amy Bayer, "Congressional Exemptions Scrutinized," *Telegram & Gazette*, November 13, 1989, A6.

p. 91, "A full cost analysis of this . . .": DeParle, "Realizing the Rights of the Disabled," December 17, 1989.

pp. 91–92, "People with disabilities packed . . .": Young, "Equality of Opportunity," July 26, 1997.

p. 92, "The subcommittee held four . . .": Young, "Equality of Opportunity," July 26, 1997.

pp. 92–93, "ADA will help provide for the . . .": U.S. Congress, *Congressional Record*, 101st Cong., 2nd sess., March 1, 1990, H571.

p. 93, "homosexuals or drug addicts": Amy Bayer, "AIDS Exclusion Struck from Rights Bill," *Telegram & Gazette*, March 14, 1990, C2.

p. 93, "The *Gazette Telegraph* in Colorado . . .": Dave Curtin, "GT Editorial Cartoon Spurs Protest by Disabled," *Gazette Telegraph*, April 6, 1990, B1.

p. 94, "It's like taking an article on child . . .": Laura A. Kieman, "Alliance Irked at Douglas Letter," *Boston Globe*, April 8, 1990, 2.

p. 94, "another giant leap toward floor . . .": U.S. Congress, *Congressional Record*, 101st Cong., 2nd sess., March 15, 1990, H842.

p. 96, "Transportation issues posed . . .": Young, "Equality of Opportunity," July 26, 1997.

p. 96, "injure the bill 'in any way'": Gary Washburn, "METRA Wins Round on Disabled Bill," *Chicago Tribune*, March 7, 1990, 3.

p. 97, "We're here to send . . .": Steven A. Holmes, "Measure Barring Discrimination Against Disabled Runs Into Snag," *New York Times*, March 13, 1990, 1.

p. 98, "It is a bill whose time . . .": "Rights for Disabled," *Newsday*, May 18, 1990, 14.

p. 99, "Jim Crow amendment of 1990 . . .": "House Vote on Food Handlers With AIDS," *San Francisco Chronicle*, May 18, 1990, A14. Retrieved October 27, 2009, from ProQuest Newsstand. (Document ID: 67591971).

p. 99, "the most sweeping civil rights . . .": Steven A. Holmes, "House Approves Bill Establishing Broad Rights for Disabled People," *New York Times*, May 23, 1990, 1.

p. 99, "an American milestone . . .": John Kemp and Bob Williams, "Disabilities Act an American Milestone," *Austin American Statesman*, July 31, 1990, A11.

p. 99, "If you're going to have . . .": Bob Minzesheimer, "House OKs Disabilities Act," *USA Today*, May 23, 1990, 04A.

p. 100, "I could taste the freedom . . .": McInnis-Misenor, interview with the author.

p. 100, "I envision a day . . .": Betsy Wade, "Practical Traveler; A Bill of Rights for the Disabled Nears Passage," *New York Times*, December 17, 1989.

p. 100, "You can't legislate attitudes . . .": Steven A. Holmes, "The Disabled Find a Voice, and Make Sure It Is Heard," *New York Times*, March 18, 1990.

p. 101, "codify ignorance": "Senate Joins House in Ban on Food Workers With AIDS," *Austin American Statesman,* June 7, 1990, A9. Retrieved October 27, 2009, from ProQuest Newsstand. (Document ID: 82649973).

p. 101, "right to the heart and soul . . .": U.S. Congress, *Congressional Record*, 101st Cong., 2nd sess., June 6, 1990, S7437.

p. 101, "Fifty years ago, people . . .": Kevin Cullen, "Panel Drops AIDS Curb in Disability Rights Bill," *Boston Globe*, June 26, 1990, 3.

pp. 101–102, "It was a tough call for some . . .": Young, "Equality of Opportunity," July 26, 1997.

p. 102, "Disability rights activists Wright and Robert Silverstein . . .": Young, "Equality of Opportunity," July 26, 1997.

pp. 102–103, "We send a loud message that we . . .": U.S. Congress, *Congressional Record*, 101st Cong., 2nd sess., July 11, 1990, S9533.

p. 103, "We stand poised on the threshold . . .": U.S. Congress, *Congressional Record*, 101st Cong., 2nd sess., July 12, 1990, H4615.

p. 103, "the hope bill . . .": U.S. Congress, *Congressional Record*, July 12, 1990, H4622.

p. 103, "We are on the brink of . . .": U.S. Congress, *Congressional Record*, July 12, 1990, H4628.

p. 104, "This bill, in large measure . . .": U.S. Congress, *Congressional Record*, July 12, 1990, H4630.

p. 104, "every Senator in this Chamber . . .": U.S. Congress, *Congressional Record*, 101st Cong., 2nd sess., July 13, 1990, S9685.

p. 104, "I did my job . . .": U.S. Congress, *Congressional Record*, July 13, 1990, S9687.

p. 104, "today was my proudest day . . .": U.S. Congress, *Congressional Record*, July 13, 1990, S9689.

p. 105, "go to the farthest lengths . . .": U.S. Congress, *Congressional Record*, July 13, 1990, S9694.

p. 105, "Honey, you're part of history . . .": McInnis-Misenor, interview with author.

pp. 105–106, "the world's first declaration . . .": Young, "Equality of Opportunity," July 26, 1997.

p. 106, "one of the most important . . .": Rasky, "How the Disabled Sold Congress on a New Bill of Rights," September 17, 1989.

p. 107, "could be expected to take care . . .": Evan J. Kemp Jr., "A Letter from Evan J. Kemp, Jr.," U.S. EEOC, www.eeoc.gov/abouteeoc/35th/voices/kemp.html.

p. 107, "This is what's so great about . . .": McInnis-Misenor, interview with author.

Chapter Six

p. 109, "We changed thousands of lives, . . .": Marcelle S. Fischler, "The Dearly Departed, Class of '04; Henry Viscardi Jr.—Employing the Disabled," *New York Times,* December 26, 2004.

p. 109, "When the law was passed in 1990 . . .": Susan F. Rasky, "How the Disabled Sold Congress on a New Bill of Rights," *New York Times*, September 17, 1989, Week in Review.

p. 110, "A Harris poll conducted in 2003 . . .": Steven Greenhouse, "Pursuing a Chance in a Hard Job Market," *New York Times*, June 15, 2003, New York Region, 1.

p. 110, "If you're competent, then your . . .": Steven Greenhouse, "Pursuing a Chance in a Hard Job Market," June 15, 2003.

pp. 110–111, "Computers that talk . . .": Sheryl Burgstahler, "Working Together: People with Disabilities and Computer Technology," Do-It, University of Washington: 2008, www.washington.edu/doit/Brochures/Technology/wtcomp.html.

p. 111, "The computer is allowing us to . . .": Peter H. Lewis, "A Great Equalizer for the Disabled," *New York Times*, November 6, 1988, Technology.

p. 111, "In February 2006 . . .": Miguel Helft, "For the Blind, Technology Does What a Guide Dog Can't," *New York Times*, January 3, 2009, BU1.

p. 112, "A study conducted in 2003 . . .": Lynnley Browing, "Personal Business; From Beaches to Cities, Efforts to Serve Disabled Travelers," *New York Times*, October 19, 2003.

p. 112, "The worst place on earth . . .": Lynnley Browing, "Personal Business," October 19, 2003.

p. 113, "You didn't really want to . . .": Rus Cooper-Dowda, "Off the Bus," *Ragged Edge Online*, 2000, www.raggededgemagazine.com/extra/offthebus.htm.

p. 114, "under savage attack in the . . .": "Tony Coelho Issues 'Work Agenda Challenge' to 2004 Presidential Hopefuls," Epilepsy Foundation, October 24, 2003, www.epilepsyfoundation.org/epilepsyusa/coelhonylsaddress.cfm.

p. 114, "any physical or mental impairment.": National Council on Disability, *Righting the ADA*, December 1, 2004.

p. 114, "By January 2008, . . .": Chai R. Feldblum, Kevin Barry, and Emily A. Benfer, "The ADA Amendments Act of 2008," Georgetown University's Archive: ADA: The Path to Equality, www.archiveADA.org.

p. 116, "restore the original promise and . . .": Tom Harkin, "Senator Harkin's Statement Regarding ADA Amendments Act Becoming Law," U.S. Senate, September 25, 2008, http://harkin.senate.gov/blog/?i=71901158-8932-40c5-a107-4f6e92cc59b7.

p. 116, "FILING A DISCRIMINATION COMPLAINT": "Charge Statistics FY 1997 Through FY 2008," U.S. EEOC. www.eeoc.gov/stats/charges.html; "Americans with Disabilities Act of 1990, ADA Charges . . . FY 1997–FY 2008," U.S. EEOC, www.eeoc.gov/stats/ada-charges.html; "Workplace Issues—Winning Discrimination Cases," Social Issues Reference, http://social.jrank.org/pages/784/Workplace-Issues-Winning Discrimination-Cases.html; and U.S. EEOC, "Performance Results," www.eeoc.gov/abouteeoc/plan/par/2008/performance_results.html#litigation_results.

p. 116, "From October 1, 2007, . . .": "Americans with Disabilities Act," U.S. EEOC, www.eeoc.gov/types/ada.html.

p. 117, "If the EEOC rules . . .": Kelly Pate Dwyer, "Taking Action Against Discrimination," *New York Times*, October 2, 2005, Job Market section.

p. 117, "Freedom is a constant struggle . . .": Kathryn McInnis-Misenor, interview with the author, October 1, 2008.

p. 117, "all of the hospital's labor and delivery . . .": Jessica Balkun Begley, OB Parent Education Program manager, Family Birth Center, Maine Medical Center, e-mail message to author, July 1, 2009.

p. 118, "Filing a Claim": U.S. EEOC, "Filing a Charge of Employment Discrimination," December 20, 2007, www.eeoc.gov/charge/overview_charge_filing.html; U.S. Department of Justice, "A Guide to Disability Rights Laws," September 2005, www.ada.gov/cguide.htm#anchor62335; Kelly Pate Dwyer, "Taking Action Against Discrimination," *New York Times*, October 2, 2005, http://query.nytimes.com/gst/fullpage.html?res=9E06EFDB1030 F931A35753C1A9639C8B63; and Lesley Alderman, "How to Proceed With a Complaint," *New York Times*, March 27, 2009, www.nytimes.com/2009/03/28/health/28patientside.html?scp=1&sq="How%20to%20Proceed%20With%20a%20Complaint,"%20&st=cse.

p. 119, "Laws can do a lot, . . .": McInnis-Misenor, interview with the author.

p. 119, "If you talk the talk . . .": McInnis-Misenor, interview with the author.

p. 119, "'That fact,' said McInnis-Misenor, 'is now embedded . . .'": McInnis-Misenor, interview with the author.

pp. 120–123, "From Bill to Law": Senate workload, 1947–2000, www.congresslink. org/print_basics_histmats_workloadstats.htm; House workload, 1947–2000, www. congresslink.org/print_basics_histmats_workloadstats; and Charles W. Johnson, "How Our Laws Are Made," Washington, D.C.: U.S. Government Printing Office, 1998.

All websites accessible as of September 17, 2009.

Further Information

AUDIO/VIDEO

Gibson, William. *The Miracle Worker*. DVD. Directed by Arthur Penn. Playfilm Productions, 1962.

The Legislative Branch. DVD. Schlessinger Media, 2002.

MacGowan, Paul. *Speak Out for Understanding*. DVD. Directed by Paul MacGowan. Video Expeditions, 2008.

Real Life Teens: Teens & Disabilities. DVD. TMW Media Group, 2008.

BOOKS

Banks, Joan. *The U.S. Constitution*. Broomall, PA: Chelsea House Publications, 2001.

Barber, Benjamin R. *A Passion for Democracy*. Princeton, NJ: Princeton University Press, 2000.

Charlton, James I. *Nothing About Us Without Us: Disability Oppression and Empowerment*. Berkeley: University of California Press, 2000.

Goren, William D. *Understanding the Americans with Disabilities Act*, 2nd ed. Chicago: American Bar Association, 2007.

Hamilton, Lee H. *How Congress Works and Why You Should Care*. Bloomington: Indiana University Press, 2004.

Johnson, Mary, and Barrett Shaw. *To Ride the Public's Buses: The Fight That Built a Movement*. Disability Rag Reader. Louisville, KY: Advocado Press, 2001.

Kaufman, Miriam. *Easy for You to Say: Q and As for Teens Living With Chronic Illness or Disabilities*, rev. ed. Richmond Hill, Ontario: Firefly Books, 2005.

Kent, Deborah, and Kathryn A. Quinlan. *Extraordinary People With Disabilities*. Danbury, CT: Children's Press, 1997.

Longmore, Paul, and Lauri Umansky. *The New Disability History: American Perspectives*. New York: New York University Press, 2001.

O'Brien, Ruth, ed. *Voices from the Edge: Narratives about the Americans with Disabilities Act*. New York: Oxford University Press, 2004.

Switzer, Jacqueline Vaughn. *Disabled Rights: American Disability Policy and the Fight for Equality*. Washington, D.C.: Georgetown University Press, 2003.

Thornton, Denise. *Physical Disabilities: The Ultimate Teen Guide*. Lanham, MD: The Scarecrow Press, 2007.

WEBSITES

The American Association of People with Disabilities
www.aapd-dc.org/

Disability Rights Advocates
www.dralegal.org/

Disability Rights Education & Defense Fund
www.dredf.org/ADA.shtml

Disability Rights Legal Center
www.disabilityrightslegalcenter.org/

Disability Statistics Center
www.dsc.ucsf.edu/main.php

Georgetown University's ArchiveADA: The Path to Equality
www.archiveADA.org

Mountain State Centers for Independent Living: History of the ADA
www.mtstcil.org/skills/ada1-b.html

National Council on Disability
www.ncd.gov/newsroom/publications/1997/equality.htm

National Institute on Disability and Rehabilitation Research
www.adata.org

U.S. Department of Justice: Americans with Disabilities Act
www.ada.gov/

U.S. Equal Employment Opportunity Commission (EEOC) ADA site
www.eeoc.gov/abouteeoc/35th/history/index.html

Bibliography

ARTICLES

Associated Press. "Appeals Court Orders That Buses Be Fitted for Handicapped." *New York Times*, February 14, 1989.

———. "Convention in Dallas: The Republicans; Excerpts from Platform Adopted by Republican Convention." *New York Times*, August 22, 1984.

———. "Handicapped in Protest of 'Federalism' Policy." *New York Times*, May 1, 1982.

———. "New England News in Brief; Bus-Access Order Won by Handicapped." *Boston Globe*, August 15, 1984: 1.

Bayer, Amy. "AIDS Exclusion Struck from Rights Bill." *Telegram & Gazette,* March 14, 1990: C2.

———. "Congressional Exemptions Scrutinized." *Telegram & Gazette*, November 13, 1989: A6.

Beeder, David C. "Disabilities Act Near Hearings; Some Opposed." *Omaha–World Herald,* September 6, 1989: 10.

Brady, James S. "Save Money: Help the Disabled." *New York Times*, August 29, 1989: op-ed page.

Browing, Lynnley. "Personal Business; From Beaches to Cities, Efforts to Serve Disabled Travelers." *New York Times*, October 19, 2003.

Burgstahler, Sheryl. "Working Together: People with Disabilities and Computer Technology." Do-It, University of Washington, 2008, www.washington.edu/doit/Brochures/Technology/wtcomp.html.

"Bush Signs Bill to Outlaw Bias Against Disabled." *Austin American Statesman,* July 27, 1990: A1.

Coelho, Tony. "Tony Coelho Issues 'Work Agenda Challenge' to 2004 Presidential Hopefuls." Epilepsy Foundation, October 24, 2003. www.epilepsyfoundation.org/epilepsyusa/coelhonylsaddress.cfm.

Cooper-Dowda, Rus. "Off the Bus." *Ragged Edge Magazine*, 2000, www.raggededgemagazine.com/extra/offthebus.htm.

Cullen, Kevin. "Panel Drops AIDS Curb in Disability Rights Bill." *Boston Globe*, June 26, 1990: 3.

Curtin, Dave. "GT Editorial Cartoon Spurs Protest by Disabled." Colorado Springs *Gazette Telegraph*, April 6, 1990: B1.

Dart, Justin. "ADA: Landmark Declaration of Equality." *Worklife*, September 22, 1990.

DeParle, Jason. "Ideas & Trends; Realizing the Rights of the Disabled." *New York Times*, December 17, 1989: Week in Review.

DeParle, Jason. "Realizing the Rights of the Disabled." *New York Times*, December 17, 1989: 1A.

"Disability Bill to Cost Millions." *New York Times*, August 14, 1989.

"Disabled Tie Up Traffic Here to Protest Nixon Aid-Bill Vote." *New York Times*, November 3, 1972: 43.

Dwyer, Kelly Pate. "Taking Action Against Discrimination." *New York Times*, October 2, 2005: Job Market section.

Editorial. "A Hollow Victory." *New York Times*, April 11, 1977: 12.

Editorial. "The Lawyers' Employment Act." *Wall Street Journal*, September 11, 1989: 1.

Editorial. "McInnis: Her Legal Rights of Access." *Journal Tribune*, November 13, 1980: 4.

Elder, Janet. "Disabled View Their Gains." *New York Times*, May 21, 1986.

Farrell, Mary Ann. "Justin Dart Widely Acclaimed as Leading Advocate for Disabled Rights Movement." Knight-Ridder/Tribune News Service, June 10, 1994.

Fay, Fred, and Fred Pelka, "Justin Dart—An Obituary." Disability Social History Project, June 22, 2002, www.disabilityhistory.org/people_dart.html.

Feldblum, Chai R., Kevin Barry, and Emily A. Benfer. "The ADA Amendments Act of 2008." Georgetown University's ArchiveADA: The Path to Equality. www.archiveADA.org.

Fischler, Marcelle S. "The Dearly Departed, Class of '04; Henry Viscardi Jr.—Employing the Disabled." *New York Times*, December 26, 2004.

Flint, Jerry. "Civil Rights: Handicapped No Longer Act Like It." *New York Times*, October 2, 1977: E8.

French, Kimberly. "Samuel Gridley Howe: Champion of the Blind." *UU World*, January/February 2005, Unitarian Universalist Association.

Giroux, Gerald E. "Support for Councilor McInnis." *Journal Tribune*, November 13, 1980: 4.

Gold, John. "Maine Disabled Woman Wheels Way to Success." *Journal Tribune*, March 2, 1987: 10.

Greenhouse, Linda. "Deaf Student Loses High Court Appeal," *New York Times*, June 12, 1979: 1.

Greenhouse, Steven. "Pursuing a Chance in a Hard Job Market." *New York Times*, June 15, 2003: New York/Region-1.

Helft, Miguel. "For the Blind, Technology Does What a Guide Dog Can't." *New York Times*, January 3, 2009: BU1.

Hicks, Nancy. "Berkeley Turns into Mecca for Handicapped Persons." *New York Times*, September 8, 1976: 16.

——. "Califano Signs Regulations to Ban Discriminations Against Disabled." *New York Times*, April 29, 1977: NJ1.

——. "Handicapped Use Protests to Push H.E.W. to Implement '73 Bias Law." *New York Times*, April 29, 1977: NJ1.

Holmes, Steven A. "House Approves Bill Establishing Broad Rights for Disabled People." *New York Times,* May 23, 1990: 1.

——. "Measure Barring Discrimination Against Disabled Runs Into Snag." *New York Times*, March 13, 1990: 1.

——. "The Nation: The Disabled Find a Voice, and Make Sure It Is Heard." *New York Times*, March 18, 1990.

"House Vote on Food Handlers with AIDS." *San Francisco Chronicle*, May 18, 1990: A14.

"House/Senate Workload, 1947–2000." www.congresslink.org/print_basics_histmats_workloadstats.htm.

Hoyt, Austin. "Ronald Reagan, 40th President," *American Experience*. Public Broadcasting Service, 1998, www.pbs.org/wgbh/amex/presidents/40_reagan/reagan_domestic.html.

Hunter, Marjorie. "Congress Votes Bill Facing Veto; Aid to Handicapped Children Chosen for Initial Test of Strength." *New York Times,* March 16, 1973: 19.

Johnson, Allen F. "ADA Protects Rights of the Disabled." *Telegram & Gazette*, March 19, 1990: D1.

Johnson, Charles W. *How Our Laws Are Made*, Washington, D.C.: U.S. Government Printing Office, 1998.

"Justin Dart Jr. Legend in Disabilities Advocacy." *The Exceptional Parent*, August 1, 2002.

Kemp, Evan J. Jr. "A Letter from Evan J. Kemp, Jr." Equal Employment Opportunity Commission. www.eeoc.gov/abouteeoc/35th/voices/kemp.html.

Kemp, John, and Bob Williams. "Disabilities Act an American Milestone." *Austin American Statesman*, July 31, 1990: A11.

Kieman, Laura A. "Alliance Irked at Douglas Letter." *Boston Globe*, April 8, 1990: 2.

Koblert, Elizabeth. "As Candidate, Dole Casts Off His Feats as a Skilled Senator." *New York Times*, August 9, 1996: 1.

"Koch Blocks Accord on Subway Access for Disabled People." *New York Times*, June 22, 1984.

Letters to the Editor. *Journal Tribune*, November 8, 9, 10, 13, 1980: 4.

Leuck, Thomas J. "The New Teeth in the Fair Housing Law." *New York Times*, March 12, 1989.

Lewis, Peter H. "A Great Equalizer for the Disabled." *New York Times*, November 6, 1988: Technology.

Maeroff, Gene I. "Quandary for the Colleges: Law Barring Discrimination Against Handicapped Could Force Expensive Alterations on Campus." *New York Times*, June 16, 1979: 19.

Marquard, Bryan. "Charlie Sabatier; Helped Win Access, Respect for Disabled." *Boston Globe*, June 12, 2009, www.boston.com/bostonglobe/obituaries/articles/2009/06/12/charlie_sabatier_helped_win_access_respect_for_disabled.

Mayerson, Arlene. "The History of the ADA: A Movement Perspective." Disability Rights Education and Defense Fund, 1992, www.dredf.org/publications/ada_history.shtml.

McInnis, Kathryn. "Letter to the Editor." *Journal Tribune*, November 11, 1980: 4.

Minzesheimer, Bob. "House OKs Disabilities Act." *USA Today*, May 23, 1990: 04A.

Molotsky, Irvin. "House and Senate Vote to Override Reagan on Rights." *New York Times*, March 23, 1988: 1.

Mutchler, Meghan. "Roosevelt's Disability an Issue at Memorial." *New York Times*, April 10, 1995.

News Services. "Springs Women See 'Independence Day'/ Bush Signs Law to Aid Handicapped." *Gazette-Telegraph*, July 27, 1990: A1.

Povich, Elaine S. "Senate OKs Bill Fixing Rights of the Disabled." *Chicago Tribune*, July 14, 1990: 1.

Rasky, Susan F. "Bill Barring Bias Against Disabled Holds Wide Impact." *New York Times*, August 14, 1989.

——. "How the Disabled Sold Congress on a New Bill of Rights." *New York Times,* September 17, 1989: Week in Review.

——. "Senate Adopts Sweeping Measure to Protect Rights of the Disabled." *New York Times*, September 8, 1989: 1.

"Rights for Disabled," *Newsday*, May 18, 1990: 14.

"Rights for the Disabled: White House Backs Bill to Prohibit Discrimination." *Austin American Statesman*, June 23, 1989: 4A.

Robbins, Gary L. "Brand-new Saco Councilor at Center of City Hall Uproar." *Journal Tribune*, November 6, 1980: 10.

——. "Councilor Wins Fight to Change Meeting Places." *Journal Tribune*, November 25, 1980: 1.

Roberts, Steven V. "The Handicapped Are Emerging as a Vocal Political Action Group." *New York Times*, June 19, 1978: A16.

Saddler, Jeanne. "Small Firms Lobby to Revise Bill Helping the Disabled," *Wall Street Journal*, February 23, 1990: B2.

——. "Small Firms Say Law Would Hit Them Hardest." *Wall Street Journal,* May 23, 1990: B1.

"Senate Joins House in Ban on Food Workers with AIDS." *Austin American Statesman*, June 7, 1990: A9.

Stone, Karen G. "Justin Dart, Jr.—A Peek of Insight." Independent Living Institute, February 2001, www.independentliving.org/column/stone200102.html.

"The House." *Los Angeles Times*, May 24, 1990: 6.

"The House: Transmittable Diseases." *Los Angeles Times*, May 25, 1990: 6.

Thornburgh, Dick. "Toward Independence for the Disabled." *Wall Street Journal*, October 6, 1989: 1.

Tolchin, Martin. "Civil Rights Plan Shelved as Senate Moves on Spending." *New York Times*, October 3, 1984: 1.

U.S. Department of Veterans Affairs. "History of the Department of Veterans Affairs—Part 1." February 11, 2008, www1.va.gov/opa/feature/history/history1.asp.

U.S. Holocaust Memorial Museum. "The Nazi Persecution of Deaf People." www.ushmm. org/museum/exhibit/focus/disabilities_02.

U.S. Office of Special Programs. "History: Twenty-Five Years of Progress in Educating Children with Disabilities Through IDEA." Washington, D.C.: U.S. Department of Education, 2000, www.ed.gov/policy/speced/leg/idea/history.pdf.

Wade, Betsy. "Practical Traveler; A Bill of Rights for the Disabled Nears Passage." *New York Times*, December 17, 1989.

Waldman, Myron S. "A Bill of Rights for the Disabled: House OKs Antidiscrimination Act." *Newsday*, May 23, 1990: 1.

Washburn, Gary. "METRA Wins Round on Disabled Bill." *Chicago Tribune*, March 7, 1990: 3.

"Workplace Issues—Winning Discrimination Cases." Social Issues Reference, http://social. jrank.org/pages/784/Workplace-Issues-Winning-Discrimination-Cases.html.

Yee, Silvia, and Marilyn Golden. "Achieving Accessibility: How the Americans with Disabilities Act Is Changing the Face and Mind of a Nation." Disability Rights Education & Defense Fund, www.dredf.org/international/paper_y-g.html#_ftn114.

Young, Jonathan M. "Equality of Opportunity: The Making of the Americans with Disabilities Act." National Council on Disability, July 26, 1997. www.ncd.gov/newsroom/ publications/1997/equality.htm.

Books

Elliott, Maud Howe, and Florence Howe Hall. *Laura Bridgman: Dr. Howe's Famous Pupil and What He Taught Her*. Boston: Little, Brown, and Company, 1903.

Goffman, Erving. *Stigma: Notes on the Management of Spoiled Identity*. New York: Simon & Schuster, 1963.

Harris, James C. *Intellectual Disability: Understanding its Development, Causes, Classification, Evaluation, and Treatment*. New York: Oxford University Press, 2006.

Johnson, Mary, and Barrett Shaw. *To Ride the Public's Buses: The Fight That Built a Movement*. Disability Rag Reader. Louisville, KY: Advocado Press, 2001.

Longmore, Paul K. *Why I Burned My Book and Other Essays on Disability*. Philadelphia: Temple University Press, 2003.

Myers, John E. B. *Child Protection in America: Past, Present, and Future*. New York: Oxford University Press, 2006.

Court Cases

Alexander v. Choate, 469 U.S. 287, 1985.

Americans Disabled for Accessible Public Transportation v. Burnley, 881 F.2d 1184, 58 USLW 2090, July 24, 1989.

Consolidated Rail Corporation v. Darrone, 465 U.S. 627, 1984.

School Board of Nassau County, Florida, et al. v. Arline, 480 U.S. 273, 1987.

Southeastern Community College v. Davis, 442 U.S. 397, 1979.

Interviews

Begley, Jessica Balkun. E-mail Interview by Susan Dudley Gold. July 1, 2009.

McInnis-Misenor, Kathryn. Interview by Susan Dudley Gold. October 1, 2008.

Sawisch, Leonard. E-mail Interview by Susan Dudley Gold. October 15, 2008.

Sawtelle, Kenneth. Interview by Susan Dudley Gold. September 1996.

Public Documents

Bush, George H. W. "Remarks of President George Bush at the Signing of the Americans with Disabilities Act." U.S. Equal Employment Opportunity Commission, www.eeoc.gov/ abouteeoc/35th/videos/ada_signing_text.html.

Clinton, William. "President's Remarks on Justin Dart Jr." Independent Living Research Utilization, January 15, 1998, www.ilru.org/html/about/Dart/remarks.html.

——. "Remarks on the Unveiling of a Statue at the Franklin D. Roosevelt Memorial." Washington, D.C., January 10, 2001, www.presidency.ucsb.edu/ws/index.php?pid=65051.

Grizzard, W. Roy. "Impact of Disability History, Identity and Community—Yesterday, Today and Tomorrow." Speech, 2004 National Youth Leadership Conference, U.S. Department of Labor Office of Disability Employment Policy, July 26, 2004, www.dol.gov/odep/media/speeches/youth.htm.

Harkin, Tom. "Senator Harkin's Statement Regarding ADA Amendments Act Becoming Law." Tom Harkin's Web Site, September 25, 2008, http://harkin.senate.gov/blog/?i=71901158-8932-40c5-a107-4f6e92cc59b7.

——. "Senator Tom Harkin in Supporting Nomination of Judy Heumann as Assistant Secretary for Special Education and Rehabilitative Services." U.S. Congress, Senate, *Congressional Record*, 103rd Cong., 1st sess., June 23, 1993, S7738.

National Policy for Persons with Disabilities. National Council on Disability, 1984, www.ncd.gov/newsroom/publications/1984/nationalpolicy_1984.htm.

Righting the ADA. National Council on Disability, December 1, 2004, www.ncd.gov/newsroom/publications/2004/pdf/righting_ada.pdf.

Toward Independence: An Assessment of Federal Laws and Programs Affecting Persons with Disabilities — With Legislative Recommendations. National Council on Disability, February 1986, www.ncd.gov/newsroom/publications/1986/toward.htm.

U.S. Congress. *Americans with Disabilities Act of 1990*. 101st Cong., 2nd sess., 1990.

——. *Congressional Record*, 100th Cong., 1st–2nd sess., 1987–1988.

——. *Congressional Record*, 101st Cong., 1st–2nd sess., 1989–1990.

——. *Congressional Record*, 103rd Cong., 1st–2nd sess., 1993–1994.

——. *Rehabilitation Act of 1973, Public Law 93-112*, 93rd Cong., H. R. 8070, 1973.

WEBSITES

CongressLink, The Dirksen Congressional Center
www.congresslink.org

Disability Rights Education & Defense Fund
www.dredf.org/ADA.shtml

Disability Rights Legal Center
www.disabilityrightslegalcenter.org/

Georgetown University's ArchiveADA: The Path to Equality
www.archiveADA.org

National Council on Disability
www.ncd.gov/newsroom/publications/1997/equality.htm

U.S. Department of Justice: Americans with Disabilities Act
www.ada.gov/

U.S. Equal Employment Opportunity Commission
www.eeoc.gov

U.S. EEOC ADA site
www.eeoc.gov/abouteeoc/35th/history/index.html

All websites accessible as of September 17, 2009.

Index

Page numbers in **boldface** are illustrations, tables, and charts.

About the Author

SUSAN DUDLEY GOLD has worked as a reporter for a daily newspaper, managing editor of two statewide business magazines, and freelance writer for several regional publications. She has written more than four dozen books for middle-school and high-school students on a variety of topics, including American history, health issues, law, and space.

Gold has won numerous awards for her work, including most recently the selection of Loving *v.* Virginia*: Lifting the Ban Against Interracial Marriage*, part of Marshall Cavendish's Supreme Court Milestones series, as one of the Notable Social Studies Trade Books for Young People in 2009. Two other books in that series were recognized in 2008: United States *v.* Amistad: *Slave Ship Mutiny,* selected as a Carter G. Woodson Honor Book, and Tinker *v.* Des Moines: *Free Speech for Students*, awarded first place in the National Federation of Press Women's communications contest, nonfiction juvenile book category.

Gold has written several titles in the Landmark Legislation series for Marshall Cavendish. She is the author of several books on Maine history. She and her husband, John Gold, own and operate a web design and publishing business in Maine. They have one son, Samuel, and a granddaughter, Callie.